they called me

white
jesus

bill rieser

with bruce nygren

they called me

white jesus

I was a legend . . . now I'm something more

MOODY PUBLISHERS

CHICAGO

The material presented in this book is not intended to replace professional counsel. Neither the publisher nor the author assumes responsibility for adverse consequences resulting from application of advice presented here.

Edited by: Jim Vincent
Interior Design: Ragont Design
Cover Design: The DesignWorks Group

Library of Congress Cataloging-in-Publication Data

Rieser, Bill.
  They called me White Jesus : I was a legend-- now I'm something more /
Bill Rieser with Bruce Nygren.
    p. cm.
  ISBN 978-0-8024-2298-9
  1. Rieser, Bill. 2. Christian biography--United States. I. Nygren,
Bruce. II. Title.
  BR1725.R572A3 2009
  277.3'083092--dc22
  [B]
                          2008054845

We hope you enjoy this book from Moody Publishers. Our goal is to provide high-quality, thought-provoking books and products that connect truth to your real needs and challenges. For more information on other books and products written and produced from a biblical perspective, go to www.moodypublishers.com or write to:

Moody Publishers
820 N. LaSalle Boulevard
Chicago, IL 60610

1 3 5 7 9 10 8 6 4 2

Printed in the United States of America

To Carolynn, my wife,
who showed me the way to peace and joy.
And to Kristen, my precious daughter.

Contents

acknowledgments

I am so grateful for all the people God has placed in my life who played a part in the journey that is described in this book.

I have many people to thank, but two stand out above everyone else: Carolynn, my beloved wife, and my precious daughter, Kristen. Together they have showed me the way and offered a light for me to walk through. I am devoted to serving them, with God as my first love so I can love them the way God intended for me to love them.

I am very grateful to my beloved sisters, Ann Marie and Thea, and honored to be their brother.

I am extremely grateful for my relationship with Bruce Nygren. God has gifted Bruce in a unique way to capture the core of who I am and what I am about through his great gift of writing. I'm convinced that Bruce has captured in this book the very heartbeat of who God is and what He is about!

A special thanks to Mike Breaux, Richard Gaines, David Hysong, David Jeffares, and Max Appel for mentoring me and believing in me. I am a better man because of your love and how you have poured wisdom into this frail man.

There was a day when people called me a legend; thanks to everyone I have just mentioned, "now I am something more." All these wonderful people have directed me to the greatest One of all, Jesus Christ, to whom I will be grateful all the days of my life!

foreword

All right, I'll admit it. I'm a junkie . . . hoops junkie, that is. Every now and then I just have to get a fix. And even though I'm getting to the age where the three-point line is like an electric dog fence to me (it's painful to step inside where all the action is!), I still love to play basketball.

I still love to show up at an outdoor playground court and call "next." Still love the smell of a leather ball. Love to hold it, dribble it, spin it, pass it, and shoot it. I've been a student and a teacher of the game, coaching kids for the past twenty-five years. Whenever I get the chance, I watch the NBA, NCAA, NAIA, AAU, and 1 Streetball. Doesn't matter. I can't get enough! Told you—I'm a junkie.

My favorite player when I was a kid was Earl "the Pearl" Monroe. He was so smooth and looked like he played the game for fun, as his constant smile would indicate. Before he joined the New York Knicks, he was a legend at Rucker Park in New York City. They called him "Black Jesus" because he could do miracles with the ball. I loved Earl the Pearl, imitating his moves and trying to capture his passion for the game. He was cool and I wanted to be.

Several years later a young white guy started dominating play on the same playgrounds. They started calling him "White Jesus" because of his seemingly supernatural abilities on the asphalt.

Billy Rieser has been described by New York City hoop historians as one of the greatest players to ever play at the legendary Rucker Park. He had hops and would dunk so hard his wrists would bleed . . . and so would anyone who got in his way. He was an angry young man, taking out his pent-up aggression with an orange ball in his hands.

I met "White Jesus" years later, when all of the anger, bitterness, self-centeredness, and addictions had taken him down to rock bottom. He was this tall, handsome Italian with a very strong New York accent. He really stood out in central Kentucky where I ministered!

I was there when Billy surrendered his life to Christ, and I have watched the real Jesus absolutely transform his life.

I know the pages of this book will inspire you. This story is not the story of Billy Rieser; this is the story of the God of second chances. The One who pursues us. Loves us. Longs for us to do life with Him.

Billy leads our Celebrate Recovery Ministry these days, helping people get their lives back on track. I jokingly refer to him as "White Lazarus," because today his game "stinketh like it's been dead for four days." But his life is extraordinary! I'm so excited for you to read these pages. I know you'll find hope.

MIKE BREAUX
Pastor, Heartland Community Church, Rockford, Illinois

prologue

At my head.

And at my heart.

The guns, I mean. That's where they were pointing the guns.

Point blank. Muzzle on skin. I was twelve years old.

If you're thinking I was the innocent victim of a senseless crime, think again. I was in the middle of a drug deal gone bad. The guy I was buying for, a guy who killed people for a living, had slipped me money so I could buy drugs for him. All I had to do was walk in a brownstone, hand the cash to two men, and walk out with a small bag and change.

Not that I had a choice. He'd forced me to do this once before. And I was scared to death if I didn't do it this time, he might kill me. What I didn't know is that this guy was paying for his drugs with counterfeit money. These dealers were on to the game and was I going to pay for it with my life?

Obviously, something else happened. Otherwise, you wouldn't be reading this. That means there's more to the story. A lot more. And that's why you need to stay with me so I can tell you the *real* story of the guy they called . . .

White Jesus.

half-breed

*To understand who I am,
you have to understand
where I'm from.*

I doubt you've ever heard of me, which is OK because this book is not really about me anyway. It's about God—how He found me when I wanted nothing to do with Him. It's also about the incredible things I've seen God do since then.

But before I get to all of the "good stuff," I need to tell you some things about me and where I came from.

I was born in 1960, a decade perfect for me because I had a taste for rebellion. My family lived in a neighborhood called Second Little Italy in East Harlem, better known as Spanish Harlem, New York City. Second Little Italy was a five-block area, filled with decaying brownstones, where the most dominant employer was a family business called the Mafia. Many of the neighborhood's restaurants, candy stores, and joints were fronts for illegal activities—running of numbers, prostitution, drugs. The FBI was always filming secret videos in the hood, trying to trap the organized crime guys. As a kid I'm sure I appeared many times on-screen —unknowingly—in those fed flicks.

Second Little Italy did not have the notoriety of Little Italy in Manhattan, except for a few landmarks like Rao's Restaurant, which was four doors down from our brownstone walk-up. Rao's was a famous Mob restaurant in New York City, a tiny place seating about forty, very similar to the eating place portrayed in the movie *Goodfellas*. The current co-owner, Frank Pelligrino, had a part in the TV series *The Sopranos*—as well as *Goodfellas*. In December of 2003 there was a Mob-related shooting at Rao's, so the joke around the city was, "Let's go to Rao's for a couple of shots!" New York humor for you.

Harlem was populated predominantly by blacks and Puerto Ricans, with the streets ruled by gangs and thugs. Every day was combat—you didn't know when you would need to run, hide, or fight, but you'd better be ready for one of them. You could get killed in a place like this, and I almost did, more than once.

In Second Little Italy an Italian flag flew from more windows than the Stars and Stripes. My mom, Rosalie, was full-blooded Italian, but my dad, William, wasn't, which meant that William Rieser Jr.—me—was considered a "half-breed." Mom's Italian family had warned her not to marry a man whose "crime" was his German (and other) blood. But she loved him and followed her heart.

When I showed up, my parents and older sister, Ann Marie, lived in a fourth-floor apartment in a brownstone on 114th Street. Our place had five small rooms—two bedrooms, bath, living room, and kitchen.

Roaming the Hood

My dad left when I was a year old. My mom, who was one tough lady, used to tell the smileless joke that my father "went out to buy a pack of cigarettes and never came back." When he disappeared Mom had just given birth to my younger sister, Thea, so now Rosalie had three kids under age three to raise on her own. She did a great job of keeping us fed and under a roof, but the battle to survive consumed her.

Mom's parenting style, especially during the hot summer months, was summed up by "you better be home by 11 p.m. or else!" But when Mom was working late on some job, I'd take off. So as a little boy of twelve, I took to the streets. That's what I remember most from my childhood—roaming the hood and trying to avoid the human scum slumped on street corners and sprawled on the stoops.

Some relief came from my extended Italian family, like my uncle Dominick, who had a heart of gold but was one of many "characters" I knew back then. Some were funny or dangerous or both. Their names were clues to their uniqueness—"Johnny Babaloo" and "Vinny the Bird." Vinny had received his nickname because it was said his nose walked into the room two minutes before he did! Too funny. Another guy named Johnny was a character too, as in "bad character." More on him later.

A Trip with Uncle Dominick

I was four years old when Uncle Dominick called my mom and asked, "Could I take little Billy to a hockey game tonight?" My mother, welcoming some father-type influence for me and a little space for herself, said, "Sure, Billy would love to go to a hockey game." What Uncle didn't tell her was that this was an away game.

Dominick came by and we drove off in his car, stopping first for sandwiches at Katz's Deli on Houston Street. We then drove and drove on a highway. Dominick finally told me that the game was in Philadelphia! No problem for me—at that age I didn't know Philadelphia from the zoo!

Our New York Rangers defeated the Philadelphia Flyers 2 to 1, and I had a blast. But the drive back to New York took many hours, and with cell phones not yet available, Dominick couldn't call to tell Mom why we were late. She was going crazy when we came to our apartment at 3 a.m. Mom had the cops waiting down on the street and the whole neighborhood on alert. And she was so angry that she almost put Uncle Dominick's head in a bucket.

That fiery spirit typified my mom. She was a warrior, so if anybody messed with my sisters or me and my mother found out, she would beat the living daylights out of them. Mom worked when she could find a job and took welfare when she couldn't. Her family helped us out sometimes with food and clothing, but the Riesers were always scrounging to get by. Even as a little kid I was on the streets hustling, running football gambling slips or errands for the local mobsters, looking to make—or steal—a buck so Mom could get a few groceries.

Rage in My Fists

Roaming the streets, playing ball in the park, going to school, and watching sports on TV—that was my life. For other kids you might have added going to Mass because almost everybody was Roman Catholic. Some Italians were devout, but my family wasn't. We seldom went to church, except for midnight Mass at Christmas and Easter. For a while I was an altar boy, which I liked because I could steal sodas from the church basement where they held the bingo nights. Religion didn't matter to me and I didn't think about God much.

Because I was scrawny and not a "real Italian," I got picked on by the bullies who often lounged on our stoop. More for our safety and education than for religious reasons, Mom wanted to send us kids to the local Catholic elementary school, where most of the Italian kids learned; but without money for tuition, we went to public school instead. There most of my schoolmates were black or Puerto Rican, so I stood out.

First grade went OK but in second grade I hit trouble. Although I was thin as a pipe, I was the tallest kid in the class. The second largest kid was an African American boy named Obey (Yes, that's his actual name!) who thought I was a threat. Several times he tried to provoke a fight, but I wasn't interested until the day he called me one too many names and I knocked him flat. The school yard got quiet as Obey lay motionless on the concrete. This was the first time I felt rage in my fists.

A week later, as I was leaving school, a pack of older boys from outside our neighborhood were waiting for me beyond the school door. Two of them grabbed me and threw me to the sidewalk.

"We're Obey's friends and we're going to take care of you," one said. I wanted to run but I was cornered prey. After punching and kicking me, the leader grabbed my shirt, twisted the collar, and pushed a blade against my throat. *Was it a knife?* My mouth turned to dust, and I shook with fear. I expected to die.

"You touch Obey again and you're dead, white boy." My attacker pushed the knife tip into my neck. I felt my heart beating in my throat, the artery thumping like a bass drum.

"Cut his tongue out," a voice whispered.

The kid sticking my neck laughed. Others grabbed my arms and held me on the ground. Then someone broke a soda bottle. My mouth was pried open and my tormentor grabbed my tongue. I tried to scream but could only gurgle. I saw his eyes—slits of icy hate. When his lips stretched to smile, I noticed his thin moustache moistened by sweat.

"Owww," I moaned as glass sank into my tongue. I tasted my blood.

"See white boy bleed!" he snarled.

I wasn't so much worried now about losing my tongue as I was about dying.

"Cut him again!"

The boy did, three, maybe four times, the slices making red foam. I swallowed and choked.

Hate in My Heart

They left. I slumped against the building and cried. And inside I felt something hard swelling in my chest. I wiped my face and spit blood on the sidewalk. I could wiggle my tongue, so they'd not cut it off, but I was a bloody mess. I stopped at a water fountain and rinsed my mouth and cleaned my face, wiping away, I hoped, any evidence of blood and tears.

On the way home I still felt that tight knot in my chest. Later I would understand the word for this bitter ache: *hate*.

I couldn't hide my wound from my mom, who concluded I could not stay in that school. She worked extra jobs and the church helped with tuition so I could go to the parochial school on 116th Street, Our Lady of Mount Carmel, which was next to the Catholic church and just two blocks from our apartment.

Innocence Lost

The summer of 1972, when I was twelve, any ray of innocence still in me was extinguished by the dark side of East Harlem. The place was infested with bad characters, like the Mob guys and the Mob wannabes. Then there were the general misfits—angry teenagers already dead on the inside who found pleasure in bullying and hurting people, especially the young and weak. They carried knives and guns and were always on a short fuse. I'd seen what they could do; you didn't mess with them. If you saw these angry punks on your side of the street, you crossed over. But you couldn't avoid them if they were blocking your doorway or the gate to the park. Then you caught their attitude and lip and a few punches. This was the life I knew, so I didn't think much about it. Later I realized how fear released a constant rush of adrenaline in me.

That July afternoon was like most summer days in East Harlem. The sun scorched the concrete and asphalt until the heat burned your feet through your sneakers. My friends and I would walk to Ronnie's candy shop on 1st Avenue between 114th and 115th, pull a cold soda from the cooler, pay our 25 cents, then move along the street sipping the bottle, because if you drank too fast, the chilled liquid made your head hurt.

That afternoon I'd ended up with a friend in his apartment on 115th Street, and as I ran down the last flight of stairs and opened the door to the brownstone's entrance area, a young man stepped from the shadows and pressed a blade into my neck. My heart raced. I knew this guy—like many others in the hood who by their late teens had surrendered to the demons of the street.

"You gonna do what I want you to, Billy," he whispered, jabbing me. The steel glistened in the half dark. I was at his mercy, for at this time of day, it might be an hour or more before anyone came or left the building. In the distance I heard car horns honking and children splashing at an open fire hydrant. Here it was quiet, except for the rasp of his breath.

"Get down on your knees." I saw contempt in his eyes. *Why did he hate* me *so much*? *I hardly knew him.* Digging the knife into my neck, he unzipped and pulled down his pants.

I hated it but I did what he asked me to do, scarcely connecting what was happening with sex. No one came into the entryway to rescue me and the ordeal ended. He pushed me to the floor, dressed, and left without a word. I trembled, tears staining my cheeks. Would he return? Scrambling to my feet, I cracked the apartment door. He was gone. Shaking with shame, fear, and rage, I walked warily home along the hot streets.

I told no one what had happened. What good would it do? He might come back to cut me or maybe even hurt my mother. I fantasized for years what it would be like to catch him and slit his throat. Good thing that in the meantime I met God and surrendered my lust for revenge. But I'm getting ahead of the story. . . .

vertical
leap

2

This is what I became.

$\mathbf{I}$ 've learned that God is very kind and a Giver.

I didn't know that back in 1972, but if I'd been paying attention, I could have figured it out. That was the summer I should have had my brains blown out, but God wouldn't allow it. I didn't thank Him, though. I thought I was lucky.

Justice, Johnny Style

Johnny was one of those "characters" I mentioned earlier who, in our part of East Harlem, everybody avoided. A bad news dude. I'll give you an example of why.

One summer some thieves from another part of the city started robbing apartments in Second Little Italy. A break-in or two, and I suppose no one would have thought much about it. But these thieves were stealing on a regular basis, so Johnny decided to administer justice.

Who knows how many nights he and his buddies staked out brownstones, but as it happened, they were watching our building on 1st Avenue (by this time we'd moved) the night the robbers showed up. Bad decision by the bad guys.

Our family didn't hear anything, but when I got up that next morning, I saw blood dripping and body parts littering all four flights of the metal fire escape. Johnny and the others had surprised and killed the thieves, hacking the bodies into pieces with their blades. Because of these murders, the police showed more interest than normal and investigated. They talked to possible witnesses in the hood, but of course they all suffered memory loss. Nobody, Johnny included, was ever charged with a crime and, as you might expect, the robbery rate in Little Italy fell to zero for a long time.

The Constant Scowl

We still had to deal with Johnny, though. By the constant scowl on his face, I think this twisted, older teen was wall-to-wall hate. Once during that black summer of '72, I was dribbling my basketball down the sidewalk on 114th Street, heading for Jefferson Park to shoot hoops, when Johnny stopped me. "Hey, Billy," he said, "I need you to do something for me." I'd run errands for Johnny now and then, but this time it felt different.

"There are two guys waiting at a building on 112th Street. They're going to give you a package and some change."

Oh that's it, I thought. *This is about drugs.*

"Here's some money. Take this over and pick up a package for me." He told me the address of the brownstone. "And make sure you get the forty bucks in change. I'll be waiting here—you hurry up, Billy."

My heart pounding, I put the $100 bill in my pocket and took off. That easily I'd become a runner in a drug deal. Drugs were plentiful in East Harlem, with most of the guys roaming our streets using or pushing or both. If it wasn't a hard drug like heroin, it was marijuana. Getting wasted on weed or alcohol in the hood was like chewing bubble gum in other places. I needed to do a good job getting the package or I was toast.

Either the police would catch me or Johnny would hurt me if I somehow messed up his drug buy.

As Johnny had said, two Puerto Rican men were waiting in the hallway of the apartment building. When I told them who had sent me and handed over the money, the dealers gave me the package and two $20 bills.

I ran back to 114th, keeping a low profile, sneaking looks over my shoulder. Johnny grabbed the package and the $40 and gave me a couple of bucks as a tip. "Good," he said.

I picked up my basketball and dribbled full speed for the park.

A week later Johnny asked me to do it again. What could I say? I had heard about Johnny cracking bats on people's heads and taking out thieves with vigilante vengeance. He was the local Mafia hit guy. Johnny scared me a whole lot more than any drug dealer.

Besides, I did one drug deal before, and I knew what to expect. So I wasn't quite so fearful making a delivery this time—until I stepped into the same hallway and saw two pistols, a .38 and a .44, pointed at my head and chest. Each barrel looked like the end of a pipe.

"Did you bring more fake money, kid?" one of the men asked. He tore the $100 bill from my hand. "This ain't real."

Fake Money

So that was it: *Johnny was paying for his weed with phony money.* Counterfeiting was a specialty for the local mobsters.

"I didn't know!" I said. The drug dealers didn't believe me, and I saw their fingers twitching on the triggers. God's angels had to be there! I know He was protecting me when I needed it most. I saw the two index fingers tighten on the triggers, and one of the dealers tried to take me out. He pulled the trigger—I saw his finger move—but nothing happened, no sound of a gunshot. He looked at the gun, like it had malfunctioned, and shook his head in disgust.

"Wait, wait . . . ," I said. Without realizing it, I was about to make my first sales pitch. "You know, this weed ain't for me! This is for Johnny. He sent me here!"

Sure, I had ratted on Johnny because I needed to save my life. He might kill me later. So? I decided to use Johnny's reputation to my advantage. "Johnny's expecting me to come out. If you guys hurt me, he's going to come looking for you. If you want to live, *let me go!*" I wasn't lying. Johnny probably would have killed them; he and his crew might have mass murdered everybody in the building.

I was convincing. The guns lowered. "Don't you ever come back, kid," one said, pushing me toward the door.

"What about the package?" I said. They cursed and gave me the drugs. I left in a hurry.

Walking back to meet Johnny, my body shook with fear and anger. I'd had enough! I made a decision, right then—I wasn't going to do another drug deal ever again. I might try drugs myself, but I wasn't going to die hauling drugs. I had plans for my life, and I didn't see myself as another punk in the hood. I would get out of this place.

The Big Scold

When I saw Johnny I was so angry that I dared to get in his face: "Listen, man, these guys are on to you. They know your money is counterfeit. I didn't know it was counterfeit, but they said it was." Johnny looked at me sheepishly, kind of like a bully who loses confidence when you stand up to him on the playground.

"These guys almost killed me," I went on. "They drew two guns on me. And I don't care if you kill me right now, but I'm never doing another drug deal for you—ever, ever again."

He looked at me and said, "All right, Billy." And that was the end of it.

I'd learned a good thing and a bad thing that day: The good thing was that I could stand up for myself and survive. Fueled by all that rage and adrenaline, I'd found enough courage to talk my way out of being killed and to say no to Johnny. The bad thing was that I sensed that this power I felt from anger was a way to get what I wanted in life. For the next twenty years, I "solved" every tough situation with rage, anger, and bitterness. It worked because I usually got what Billy Rieser wanted.

Got Game

There was at least one good thing that happened when I was twelve: I discovered I could play basketball.

I had always liked sports, and during the summertime my buddies and I practically lived in Jefferson Park, which was across the street from our brownstones. Baseball was the first sport I was any good at. In the hood we gave each other nicknames, which were based on some physical feature or other quality. I was already a little crazy and could smack a baseball with power, so one day my friend Joey said to me, "We're going to call you 'Bats.'" After that I was "Billy Bats." I played center field (and sometimes first base) and could run down balls with my speed and leaping ability. When I wasn't playing baseball in Jefferson Park, I was on the asphalt courts shooting hoops from early morning until dark.

For many of us sports did more than fill up summer days: We believed that if you got really good at basketball or baseball, maybe you could get a free ride in college and even play for the big money as a pro. In a way these sports dreams were like drugs, a temporary escape from the dangerous streets, garbage-littered alleys, and the rat-filled apartments.

During sixth grade, the nuns at Our Lady of Mount Carmel Elementary School formed a boys' basketball team. Sure, I shot hoops a lot, but I wasn't that excited about it, because baseball was my sport—"Billy Bats" and all that. I decided to try out for the team mainly because I wanted to be with my friends. And I was the tallest boy in my class, even though my bones didn't have much meat.

I made the team and after several practices saw that I might do well at this. Basketball came easy for me. I had good ball handling skills and a sixth sense about where to go on the floor to score and grab rebounds. My reckless intensity helped, too. And above all, I had quick feet and could launch myself high off the floor. Very high. Our team won most of the games, and I led the team in rebounding and scoring with about twenty-five points per game.

After the season, at a school assembly a sister called me to the front. She complimented me on my basketball season and handed me a small trophy with an inscription saying I was the most valuable player on the team. All the kids clapped.

This was a big deal to me. Keep in mind I'd grown up without a dad and had struggled to survive on the streets. People weren't lining up around the block to tell me how great a kid I was, so the trophy and the attention were a special high. In fact, this was the greatest moment of my life. The applause made me feel warm inside. I took the trophy, smiled, and swaggered to my seat.

That's all it took; basketball became my obsession. One of my teachers gave me a book called *The Hawk*, the story of Connie Hawkins, an NBA player who had grown up in East Harlem. Guys like Julius Erving and Walt Frazier became my idols. I watched the New York Knicks on TV and religiously kept statistics on my favorite players.

By eighth grade I was known as a "player." I was thin but at 6'1" unusually tall for my age. I always played center because I was a white boy who *could* jump. And I dunked—the rim-rattling slams made famous in New York City ball.

I took every opportunity to find "game." In the city, playground ball is both sport and art, with an emphasis on going one-on-one, a way to play that combines basketball and hand-to-hand combat. The ball is brought up the court, and if you get your hands on it near the top of the circle, your teammates "set the stage" by clearing the lane and you do your moves and take your man to the hoop. The more clever your ball handling, showmanship, and raw force, the better. You try to humiliate your opponent, and scoring points is almost an afterthought.

Pistol Pete and I

Because of my God-given physical ability and intensity, I could do things with a basketball that people my age normally didn't do. Soon I was playing in other neighborhoods like the west side of Harlem, which was predominately black. Wherever I played, I dominated. Like one of my heroes, Pistol Pete Maravich, I played "black" even though I was a half-Italian white boy.

At the playground or in the projects, when you lost, you heard the guys talking smack and slunk off the court and got in line behind three or four teams waiting for "next." My teams won a whole lot more than we lost, so I didn't have to leave the court that often. I loved it.

For two years I attended St. Agnes Boys Catholic, located at 44th street and Grand Central Station. The following summer Anthony and Sammy Oddo, two longtime friends who played basketball with me and admired my game, helped talk me into transferring to Benjamin Franklin High School, which was closer to where I lived in Harlem. Back then the public school basketball teams in New York City got more exposure, and the Oddo brothers knew I needed the platform of Benjamin Franklin and the Public School Athletic League (PSAL) to showcase my game.

When I entered Benjamin Franklin, I was one of four white kids out of 2,500 students. The first week of school I met several guys in the halls who wanted to beat me up because I was white. I had learned how to take care of myself, and every time somebody wanted a fight, I took him down with one punch. At Franklin it wasn't long until I was known as a crazy white guy who shouldn't be messed with.

"Street Legend"?

Once practice started for the basketball season, the team learned quickly that I had game, and word spread fast in the student body of the "street legend" now attending the school. I wasn't the crazy white boy anymore.

Basketball success intoxicated me. For the first time in my life, I was accepted, admired, and sought after, and it felt great. *I was the man!* And, oddly enough, it was the blacks and Puerto Ricans who welcomed me most.

By my junior year, my play had reached such a competitive level that I became confident I'd found my ticket out of East Harlem. My growth spurt had slowed, but with a forty-four-inch vertical jump, it looked like I could leap out of the gym! I would elevate and pin the ball on the backboard a good twelve inches above the rim, but it was my intensity that made me most unique. All that anger burning inside me, fueled by my love for the game, helped me dominate on the court—whether it was an asphalt playground at the famous Rucker Park or the wood floor of a high school gym. Rucker was where the hoop kids showed their stuff, rules were often ignored (no refs here), and guys made their reps (reputations). In Rucker Park I took on the big stars of hoops in no-holds-barred street ball. Soon I developed a reputation for showing up my opponents.

Dunk Time

I loved to study Julius "Dr. J" Erving and Connie Hawkins (two guys now in the NBA Hall of Fame), where I learned the cradle dunk, cocking it back, and the tomahawk. I also liked the reverse slam. But I wouldn't dunk unless someone was there to challenge me. I wanted to dunk on people. When I was up there, I'd look down on the guy, smile on him, and slam it home.

When I dunked I shoved the ball through the rim with such force that my wrists often bled. If I could punish and humiliate my man on the court, eventually he would give up. That was my goal every time I played. Vinny Mallozzi, a *New York Times* writer who later wrote the book *Asphalt Gods*, called me the "hardest dunking white boy in the history of New York City."

People started coming to our games to see me dunk. Most of the time I got at least one slam down with such dramatic force that some spectators rushed the court to dance and celebrate. Sometimes the game would halt until order was restored. I kept up with the big stars who played in the annual Ruckers Park tournament, guys like Joe "The Destroyer" Hammond, Pookie Wilson, and Herman "Helicopter" Knowings. Just running with them and soaring above them gave me a big rep.

I know what I've just written sounds like I was terribly full of myself, which I was. But can you understand why basketball meant so much to me? It was my ultimate high. I got a bigger rush from basketball than from any drug, which is saying something because I tried most of them. I remember one night in high school when two friends and I tried to find out how many drugs we could consume in one night. So we used acid and mescaline. We did downers. We had cocaine. Marijuana. And we drank a lot of Heinekens, too.

That is a picture of Billy Rieser then—nothing done in moderation. I was out of control. God had given me an athletic gift, but I wasn't thanking Him or even giving Him some credit. I thought my coordination and speed and ability were somehow a result of something I had done. Arrogance and attitude came easy.

The Man?

Now that I was a popular jock, the girls showed up. My morals were out of control too. Sex was another way to dominate and release anger and get what I thought would fill up holes inside. And another tragic moment in my terrible 1972 hadn't helped.

That summer I was coming down the stairs in one of the brownstones one day when I ran into the neighborhood bunch of older teens I called FROA (Future Racketeers of America). These self-important thugs had informed the landlord that they needed the apartment for a while, and if he had tried to throw them out, he would have paid for it. The FROA were using the place to do drugs, do sex, do whatever.

This particular day as I walked by, the FROA were doing sex with a prostitute they'd kidnapped from the street. They were lined up in the hallway taking turns with her. Seeing me, they thought it would be funny to have me join in too. With my life in the balance if I resisted, I was told to have intercourse with this woman. I was scared, embarrassed, ashamed, horrified. This was not the way to learn anything about the beautiful act of love between a man and woman. The FROA were laughing and hooting as I stumbled out of the apartment.

I didn't tell anybody what had happened, so I dealt with all those feelings and more anger on my own.

Such an experience does not encourage a healthy appreciation of women. In high school I was at the age where I wanted to be a man, but with no dad or good male role model in my life, I assumed that manhood equaled sex. I had a sweetheart I really liked, and we had a good relationship but started having sex, which wasn't a good idea. I remember one night she was at our apartment and it got late, so I asked my mom if she could stay over. In the middle of the night we started messing around, and I heard my mom get up. I thought she would come tell us to stop but she didn't.

The next morning when Mom got up, she looked mad, so I thought the hammer was coming down. Instead she went up to my girlfriend and said, "I heard you two last night." And then Mom put her arm around my girlfriend and said, "My son's pretty good, isn't he?"

I don't think my mom was trying to push me over the moral edge, but I really didn't need any encouragement to assume I was God's answer to every young woman's dreams. All I could think was, *Billy, you've made it. You are the man.* It seemed a defining moment of my young adulthood.

I didn't know it, of course, but I was a thousand miles away from being a true man.

white jesus

3

I didn't want to know God, but He knew me and had given me a gift.

Major college recruiters showed up in force during my junior and senior years of high school. Because of the competition I played against—many of the hottest prospects in the country come from New York City—in my mind it was a "given" that I would get a full-ride college scholarship and eventually end up playing in the NBA.

St. John's University showed the most interest. The coach, Lou Carnesecca, and his main assistant, Brian Mahoney, recruited me for two years. Louie spent a number of evenings at my house eating food prepared by my mom's boyfriend, John, who was a great chef. Other schools, like UCLA, Notre Dame, Louisville, and Purdue, were interested, but I didn't know until later that the coaches at Ben Franklin High were screening calls and, without my consent, telling these other schools I "wasn't interested." I also didn't know that one of my coaches was a good friend of the coach at Centenary College in Shreveport, Louisiana, and they were concocting a deal involving some cash for both my coach and me.

My senior year I averaged twenty-two points and fifteen rebounds a game and made first team all city. My new nickname in the hood was "Billy NBA," and some people even called me "White Jesus." I'd better explain that one.

One of the greatest New York Knick players ever was Earl "the Pearl" Monroe. He was a superb ball handler and some of his moves were so "miraculous" that he was called "Black Jesus." More than a decade before I would play at Rucker Park, the Pearl showed his stuff during the 1965 summer Rucker tournament. The great Kareem Abdul-Jabbar (then a high school senior named Lew Alcindor heading for UCLA) remembers watching a game. Earl had traveled from Philadelphia, and two busloads of his fans came along. They "wailed" before the game, "Where's Jesus? Where's Black Jesus?" Abdul-Jabbar recalls in his book *Giant Steps.*

Anyway, since I was this skinny white kid from Harlem, somebody thought it would be funny to nickname me "White Jesus." Actually, I thought it was pretty cool to be compared in any way to the great Pearl who had won the NBA title with the Knicks in 1973 and later would join pro basketball's hall of fame.

Big Money and a Big Head

As it turned out, maybe I should have stayed in New York City and played ball at St. John's, but I chose to follow the money. This shames me now, but when I learned that I might get more than tuition, room and board, and books for my services, I signed on at Centenary College in Shreveport, Louisiana.

When I left for college in the summer of 1978, I was so cocky about my destiny that I thought soon I would be making big money in the NBA and playing at Madison Square Garden with the Knicks or some other pro team. My head was as big as my dream, and I had the attitude to go with it. In the meantime I would enjoy the wild side of campus life, get a degree, and make some "little money" playing college ball.

The Bible says there is pleasure in sin for a season. Little did I know that I had only one good basketball season left . . . and that my sin would be bearing its evil fruit for many years to come.

Soon after I arrived down south, I met one of Centenary's major athletic boosters. This guy was out of control. I was so cavalier about the NCAA rules that I concluded this was the way big-time college athletics worked. If somebody wanted to leave wads of bills lying around, I would find a pocket for them.

The booster arranged a summer "job" where I sat and earned $1,500 a week. Not bad. Next he told me I needed a car, so I found a guy selling a souped-up Oldsmobile Cutlass. I went back to the booster and told him the car's price was $2,000, and he pulled a money clip from his pocket and peeled off twenty $100 bills. The only problem was that I'd never driven a car and had no license. One of the assistant coaches brought me to the motor vehicle department where some arrangements had been made for my driver's test. It was a disaster: I didn't know how to steer and swerved across lanes and slammed the front wheel into the curb. The state trooper, a classic Southern good ole boy wearing a starched-stiff uniform and mirrored sunglasses, said with a drawl, "Boy, you gonna need lots of practice. Here's your license."

The booster and I had an agreement that if I scored so many points or flung down a spectacular slam during a game, afterward I would find money under the floor mat in my car. I didn't spend all the cash on myself. My mom had worked for years to barely get us by, so sending her a hundred dollar bill now and then was a big deal to me. I figured in a few years, when I was playing professional basketball, I could give her everything she'd ever wanted.

In the meantime I would do what I could, even if it meant bending the rules. So after every game, when I got to my car I'd find a pile of bills; the better I played, the more the money. Besides the points, the big-wallet booster based my pay on rebounds and blocked shots. After one particular game I dominated, there was $300 waiting in the car. (The average was $100, still big bucks in the late seventies.) I never needed anything to motivate me to play, but he thought I did, and I was glad to keep the change.

After helping my mom, I would spend the rest of my basketball "earnings" on food, alcohol, and girls.

"Play or Else"

I played well my freshman year, but a week before my sophomore season, I got drunk one night, tripped and fell, and shredded my knee. Back then the docs took the scalpel to busted knees, a much more invasive surgery than what's done now to repair torn cartilage. I came back to play too soon and could only go at about three-quarter speed. I told the coach I was hurting, and he told me to "play or else." So I chose the "else" and quit.

A sports agent, Ron Glass, who hoped to represent me when I headed for the NBA, was giving me advice. He had a good relationship with the head coach at Eastern Kentucky University in Richmond, and I was offered a full-ride scholarship there. In 1980, at midterm in my sophomore season, I transferred. I had to redshirt for a year to become eligible, so I moved into a dormitory and made new friends.

Carolynn Meets Her "Bo"

There weren't too many places to go in such a small college town, but no matter the location, if there was a party going on, I could find it. On a Thursday night the following September, I ran into a group of girls at a popular hangout. Among them was a tall, blue-eyed blonde named Carolynn Creech. I had a girlfriend back in Shreveport, so after a quick hello, I moved on. Carolynn was more interested in me—later I found out she had told her friends that night that she had spotted the man she would marry—me!

This was my sophomore year, my first year in Kentucky, and Carolynn and I started bumping into each other. That made for some funny moments, because she spoke Southeastern Kentucky English dialect while I spoke East Harlem. The first time we exchanged names and she said, "K-a-r-o-l-e-e-n," I thought she said "Karen." And when I spit out my name, "Bheel," she thought I said "Bo."

A week or two later she was looking for me at my dorm one night, asking the resident assistant at the front desk if there was a "Bo from New York" living there. The guy answered, "I don't know of any 'Bo' from

New York, but there is a 'Bill.'"

When I heard about that, I had a good laugh. I doubt that any guy named Bo has ever lived in East Harlem!

Before long we got the names straight and started spending time together, often watching TV at the student center. We were about as different as two people could be. She was quiet and laid-back; I was loud and intense. What a match! After a few months I ended my relationship in Louisiana and Carolynn and I started dating. It wasn't too much longer and we became "exclusive," a big step for me.

We'd eat at restaurants, take walks, and even visit with her girl-friends, all from her hometown of Manchester. Soon she invited me to go home to meet her family and experience the rural mountain area where she'd grown up.

Carolynn's family was conservative. They had attended a Baptist church where she had accepted Christ when she was eleven. Living away from home for the first time, though, she had strayed from a close relationship with God.

Folks in the Holler

We drove over to Clay County, Kentucky, a place so unlike East Harlem it could have been Mars. Carolynn's family lived in a "holler" outside of Manchester in a simple wood frame house surrounded by heavy woods. Carolynn introduced me to her mom, Parlee, and dad, Shade, and other than "hello" I couldn't understand a word they said! They looked confused, too, when I said, "Hows youse doin'?" So we smiled and nodded a lot and Carolynn acted as interpreter.

Talk about culture shock! We went inside the house and I saw guns everywhere—a shotgun propped in a corner of every room. I'd been around the Mafia types, drug dealers, and general thugs who carried guns in my hood, but I'd not seen shotguns and rifles used in a decorating scheme. The guns made more sense when I found out that Carolynn's ancestors included some Hatfields, as in "Hatfields and McCoys," but hunting—not feuding—was the main reason now for all the firearms.

Kentucky Talk

The front porch stretched the length of the house, and I sat there with Carolynn's dad and listened to yarn after yarn. I use the word "listen" loosely, because I didn't comprehend much. Shade would launch into something that sounded like "Whyee, yur no jes thet dawg ren ar trhee, coonnn beet howleen," and I would nod my head and try to laugh at the right time, if I thought Shade was telling a joke.

One thing I picked up was how much Shade liked former President Richard Nixon. He had met Nixon once during a presidential campaign at a Republican Party picnic in Clay County, and Nixon's demise was one of Shade's favorite topics. "Arreee thet Trickee Dhick geet bahm deel, yah thenk?" Shade was sure Nixon had received a "bum deal." I nodded my head and said, "I think you might be right. Nixon maybe got a bum deal."

I went with Carolynn often to visit her family because they always welcomed me and made me feel at home. Even when I brought a bottle of wine for dinner, they didn't complain, even though that was nearly the unpardonable sin in a good Baptist home in a dry county. I loved the friendly small talk at meals and the smell of smoke in the valley. I was welcomed as a member of the family even though Carolynn and I weren't a sure thing (or really serious . . . yet).

To the Bench

The coach, who had recruited me to Eastern Kentucky, and I got along great. During the year I redshirted, my knee healed and I could leap high again. I did well in practice scrimmages and was eager to join the varsity. But before the next season started, the coach left. The new guy and I did not click, so I headed to the bench. He played me some, but if I got creative on the floor, I was jerked from the game and lectured. I usually "lectured" him back, so my situation went south in a hurry.

And then I had one severe ankle sprain after another, followed by stress fractures in my feet and my knee acting up. My body slowly fell apart. By my senior season I was a seldom-used reserve. My attitude stunk. I didn't care anymore.

Basketball, which I'd planned as my ticket out of the hood and a path to riches, wasn't fun anymore. In fact, the game felt more like a curse.

Carolynn, though, stuck by me. I whined about the coach, and the more I whined, the more she supported me. She was my sounding board, and she was committed to me. I was drawn to her—I liked her innocence, her honesty. I knew she liked me for who I was, not who I could become. I enjoyed being with her.

My Great, Big, Crazy, Italian, Family Dinner

During spring break of my junior year, I took Carolynn up to New York to meet my mom and the rest of my crazy Italian brood. She and I were not engaged but knew marriage was in our future. Carolynn had always wanted to visit the city, so this was a great time to see the sights and meet the family.

The highlight—or maybe lowlight—of our trip was a dinner party in the Bronx my mom hosted on Easter Sunday. Italians are known for their cooking ability anyway, and to top it off, Mom had married John, a legendary chef. I told Carolynn this was a meal she'd never forget!

About thirty of the relatives—most of them had now immigrated to Long Island—show up and start drinking, talking, laughing, and eating. It is loud. Carolynn doesn't say much but watches wide-eyed as my relatives do their usual shticks. Lots of hands waving, loud talking (to Carolynn it sounded like yelling, but that's how my family talks), and wine flowing. Almost every year there's a big argument—one year one of my uncles argued about who's better, Italy or the United States.

But Carolynn's at a big Easter meal today. Before the turkey comes out, there are appetizers and three preliminary courses from my stepfather, the gourmet chef. We begin with Grandpa putting a peach slice in each glass, then adding the wine. Forty family members are gathered in two adjoining rooms. Mom sits down, but only briefly. She helps serve, pick up plates, and serves some more. She sits maybe ten minutes during the meal.

Uncle Dominick, still "out there" after all these years, as always drinks too much juice. Halfway through the six-course meal, he decides that he doesn't like the looks of Louie, my sister Thea's date.

No question—Louie is a piece of work. He's a wise guy, a "FROA." He probably has some loose ties to the Mob, and I see a gun under his shirt.

Dominick works Louie over, criticizing his clothes, his looks, his family. He calls the guy some not-so-nice names. The more the wine loosens Dominick's tongue, the worse the insults become.

Finally, Louie's had enough. He stands up, leans across the table, and sticks a finger in Dominick's face: "You shut your mouth or we're going outside, old man!" he yells.

In a blink my mom turns to the kitchen; no way is she going to let her dinner party get ruined by two guys acting like jerks—it is Easter Sunday, after all! She reemerges from the kitchen with the largest butcher knife she can find. The blade looks a foot long. Several of us men stand up to try to stop the fight, and Mom gets behind Dominick and screeches, "I'm gonna give you the sign of the cross!" She looks like Zorro with his sword, flicking the butcher knife in the air as she makes the sign of the cross in front of Dominick's face.

Carolynn Wonders...

Mom wants to chase the two men out of her house. Otherwise the china and the little kids could get hurt. The family all knows that. But Carolynn doesn't know something like this happens at nearly every family dinner. To her it looks like a murder is inevitable.

When I jump in between Louie and Dominick, Carolynn thinks I'm about to get stabbed and slips under the table.

When I saw her dive I laughed. I pulled up the tablecloth and said, "Don't worry, honey. It'll be over in fifteen minutes. You stay there until I get back." She was worried and speechless. This kind of thing didn't happen at Sunday dinners back in Kentucky.

Then the two angry men and I went outside. In the meantime, Uncle Dominick's girlfriend had called the cops because my uncle had $350 of her money in his pocket and she feared, if there was a fight, the money would disappear. Before anyone got hurt, the police arrived and sorted things out. After the guys calmed down, Louie decided to leave and the rest of us went back inside. I rescued Carolynn from under the table.

Everyone sat down at their places, and while Mom served cannoli and coffee, we started playing cards. That's our home. You can go crazy on one another, but once you say your piece, it's over. With coffee and cannoli, it's over. Now you could *feel the love.*

Carolynn shook her head and smiled. *What was she getting herself into?*

If she'd known what was ahead for us, I might have been without a girlfriend. God was hot on my trail, but it would be a long time before I surrendered.

death
of a
dream

4

My life headed toward disaster.

arolynn and I decided to marry in 1984, less than a year after Carolynn graduated. Of course, a number of my New York relatives wanted to make the trip to Kentucky for the big event. New York . . . meet Kentucky!

A few days before our wedding on April 28, I drove to the Lexington airport to pick up my family. Those who made the trip were my mom and stepdad, my sisters Ann Marie and Thea, Uncle Tony and Aunt Gilda, and my brother-in-law and best man, Michael Imbriali. We drove immediately into the Kentucky countryside to Clay County. Most in my family had never seen anything like Kentucky; to them it could have been motoring across the moon!

Twenty minutes after driving from the Lexington airport, my family had passed into the rolling Kentucky bluegrass country, with horse farms and stables dotting the land. The farther they traveled, the smaller the towns and houses. Finally they could see the signs of the coal mines, and nearby trailer houses and small wooden houses. They were a world away from New York City.

Since none of my family had met Carolynn's family before, it was quite a scene on the front porch of Carolynn's home as future in-laws and relatives got together, with the beagles swirling around, yelping, jumping, and licking the guests. Carolynn's dad and Uncle Tony connected right away, and in minutes Shade was showing him the slingshot he'd carved. Then he demonstrated to Tony how, when it was time to eat, Shade fired a walnut with the slingshot to ring the dinner bell at the end of the yard. Soon I overheard a comment from Shade about Dick Nixon's "bum deal."

Everyone was talking at once, but no matter the communication challenges, gracious hospitality and love won the day and the families got along fine.

Final Words for a Wedding

We were married at Horse Creek Baptist Church, which was pastored by Denvis Rush, an old fishing buddy of Carolynn's dad. The premarital counseling took place about fifteen minutes before the ceremony when Denvis met with me in a small room behind the sanctuary. The reverend was a nothing-fancy, what-you-see-is-what-you-get, no-nonsense country boy. Since it was a hot day and the room was stifling, Pastor Rush opened a window and spat through it before starting to lecture me: "You know, the last weddin' I done was with this cousin of mine. I told that boy, 'You can crawl out that window there right now. But if I shut that window, you going to go in there and marry that girl until death and death alone do you part!'" By now the preacher had the end of his index finger about two inches from the end of my nose. "Do you understand me, boy?"

My best man, Michael, was taking this all in. Michael's a consummate New Yorker, dashing in his tux and holding a comb in one hand and a cigarette in the other. He had never seen or heard anything like Pastor Denvis and kept muttering under his breath, "This is unbuleevable, unbuleevable!" Finally Michael started laughing and ran out into the sanctuary and yelled to our relatives, "You gotta come back here and listen to what this guy is tellin' Billy!"

I told the preacher he could shut the window because I wasn't going anywhere, but in truth I was getting in way over my head. I had no idea what a marriage covenant meant, and many hard years would go by before I became a godly husband to Carolynn.

Here Comes the Bride

Moments later, when Carolynn walked down that aisle with her dad at her side, I thought, *I am so fortunate to marry this woman. I really love Carolynn.* And when it was time for me to say my vows, my heart was racing in my chest. The words could hardly come out, I was so nervous. *I could never be a public speaker*, I thought.

After the ceremony we had some cake and punch in the church basement, before having the "real" reception at a hotel in a neighboring town. If we'd not given my Italian family the opportunity to dance and have a few drinks, they would have thought there'd been no wedding.

Carolynn and I had a driving honeymoon in Kentucky, Tennessee, and Ohio. Kentucky is beautiful in the spring, and we visited several of the lakes and scenic small towns, all framed by blooming flowers and budding trees. After the honeymoon, we moved into an apartment in the north Bronx. I thought it was nice to be back home, but I had to deal with the reality that I wasn't "White Jesus" walking on basketball water anymore.

Reawaken the Dream?

My dream of playing in the NBA was on life support, no question about that. My knee and ankles hurt, and I didn't care about playing ball anymore. I suppose deep down I still had a sliver of hope that lightning might strike, but how would I get one more chance?

A couple of years passed until the summer day when I took a walk in my mom and stepdad's Bronx neighborhood. A few blocks from their house, I passed some projects and saw several guys playing basketball at a playground. I found a ball, took some shots, and joined a pickup game. I felt pretty good and made some plays. As I was leaving, one of the guys said, "Hey, man, why don't you come back and play with us again?"

That little encouragement gave me some hope. About two weeks later I was playing again at the same playground. My legs didn't have all the old spring, but I had some game. A man stopped me beside the court and asked, "Would you want to play on my pro team? I've got a team from our radio station, 98.7 KISS-FM. We play in the best pro tournaments in the city."

I had heard of this team. They played in the Rucker Tournament and the West Fourth Street League. It was a "pro" team because the players were former professional or college players, and the competition was tough. I said yes.

It wasn't the NBA, but considering my aching knees, I played half-decent ball. I didn't bang my head on the rim like before, but I was slinging down some dunks and showing I had game. I thought that if my knees and ankles held up, maybe I could get a contract in Europe or South America, make a comeback, and finally get a shot at professional basketball in the United States.

Another Game Night in the City

Carolynn often came to my games but on one winter night, because my game was in a tough neighborhood, I went by myself. I asked Carolynn to stay home. I was about to leave the apartment when she asked, "Bill, will you be OK tonight?"

That's weird, I thought. "Yeah, why would I not be OK? I'm going to the projects to play ball."

"You be careful, OK?"

"Sure, don't worry about me. I'm with good people. No problems." I gave her a quick hug and hustled out. Running up the stairs from the basement I muttered, "What's up with her? Kentucky girl still doesn't understand the city."

I walked to my car parked on the street. Snow fell lightly, concealing the city's grime under a white covering. I dropped my gym bag in the back seat, swished the snow off the windshield with my bare hands, then took off south on Bruckner Boulevard. I drove toward the gym, cursing other drivers who I thought were moving too slowly. The streets, glowing from the lights of shop windows, streetlamps, and apartments, looked at peace—a snow in New York does that. While stopped at a light, three boys crossed in front of me, one of them clutching a basketball, its orange rumpled skin glistening from melting snowflakes. I knew they were coming from or on their way to a boys club or gym, and their smiles and shouts triggered some basketball memories.

I walked onto the court where my KISS teammates were warming up. "Hey, Billy NBA, what's happening?" one of them yelled. I smiled and pulled a ball from the bag. I stretched, dribbled while yelling at a friend in the crowd, and began to shoot, slowly moving toward the basket, relaxed and easy, warming my legs carefully.

God Watching Over Me

That's when I noticed him—a black man wearing camouflage fatigues and boots and giving me an odd look. When you grew up where I did, you never lose that instinct telling you something is wrong, that trouble is brewing and it's time to cross to the other side of the street. I didn't know what this guy's issue was, but he made me nervous.

Before the game started, I saw my friend Jimmy Boykin arrive and take his usual spot behind our bench. Jimmy and I worked together, and I knew he was leaving for vacation the next morning. Ever since my years playing at Ben Franklin High, Jimmy had been a fan of mine. "Hey, Jimmy!" I yelled as our team shed our warm-ups and walked on the court for the first half. He waved.

After the opening tip I forgot about the guy in fatigues, until the sound of two men shouting interrupted the game. The ruckus was behind our bench and got so loud that the referee blew the whistle to halt play. Jimmy and the guy in fatigues were arguing, so I ran over to "help out." The crowd, about a thousand people that night, were yelling and agitated. Ever since I was about twelve, my approach to a conflict was to step in and fix things, which meant hitting somebody so hard that he dropped like a rock.

"Leave my friend alone!" I yelled at the man in fatigues. I was cocked and about to unload on him when my teammates pulled me back. A security guard rushed in, and after some cursing, the guy was escorted from the gym. I saw the angry looks he gave Jimmy and me, but the game resumed and I forgot all about it.

We won the game easily, and after I said good-bye to Jimmy outside the building, we went our separate ways. As I headed toward the car, four men fell in behind me, nipping my heels. The hair on my neck crawled, so I walked faster. They sped up too, staying right behind me. I didn't say anything, just kept walking fast, my body tensed. I didn't like how this felt. *Why are they sticking on me like a shadow*?

The men followed me to my car and, with confused looks on their faces, watched as I opened the door, scrambled in, turned the ignition, and drove away. *What was that all about*? I thought as I accelerated down the street.

Back at our apartment I opened the door and Carolynn rushed up, her face pale.

"Hi, babe," I said, dropping my bag.

"Are you all right, Bill?"

"Yeah, I'm great. Why? Anything to eat around here?" Carolynn threw her arms around me and hugged hard. "What's going on?" I asked. I walked into the kitchen with Carolynn trailing along. She wouldn't let me out of her sight.

"So nothing happened tonight?" she asked.

"Nah."

"God told me to pray for your protection all night long."

I looked at her like she'd told me an alien was waiting in the closet. With me that kind of talk went in one ear and out the other. I was annoyed with the God business. Of late Carolynn had become more interested in spirituality and was even going to church. I didn't have time for God. He was trying to get my attention, but I didn't care about Him.

"No, nothing happened," I said. I'd already forgotten the altercation at the game and those guys following me to the car.

Carolynn slipped her arms around me. Without saying much else, we went to bed and fell asleep.

At work the next morning, a coworker said excitedly, "Billy, did you hear what happened to Jimmy last night after your game?"

"No, talk to me."

"Somebody followed him to his car and shot him five times! They've got Jimmy over at Montifiore Hospital and he's still alive!"

I knew right away who'd done this—the man in fatigues. I needed to tell the cops. I called Carolynn and told her what I'd heard.

"That's why God had me praying for you last night!" she said.

"Huh? What're you saying?"

"Remember, after you left for the game last night, God told me to start praying for you and not to stop until you came home! That's what I did."

Then I remembered the four men following me to the car. They'd been friends of that strange guy who'd tried to kill Jimmy—I knew it. He'd sent them to get me too. Why hadn't they taken me out?

"Bill, God was looking out for you last night. I know it!"

"Sure, sweetheart. I gotta go to the police station and then go see Jimmy. I'll see you later."

God watching out for me? Right. Where did she come up with this garbage? Best I could tell, nobody—including God—had ever watched out for me. I had the scars to prove it.

Our Beautiful Baby ... and a Cancer Within

In 1987 our daughter, Kristen, was born. For most people, the birth of a first child brings significant change in the family, but I wasn't any more the father type than the husband type. With a baby at home, for a few weeks I quit running around and carousing, but ultimately I did what I wanted to do and left Carolynn to take care of Kristen.

I became even more irresponsible, because with Carolynn so focused on our baby, I felt I had a "right" to be with other women. These lies had become an obsession with me. The unhappiness in my life was like a huge cancer eating me up inside. Instead of growing up, I was sinking deeper into a pit of bad attitudes and habits.

The final straw came—no surprise—on a basketball court. After a back injury, a doctor had told me I risked permanent disability if I kept playing. But to give up basketball felt like death. Who would Billy Rieser be without a basketball in his hands?

The KISS-FM All Stars met a team with a guy who had played for the University of Pittsburg. He was big—6 feet 6 and 280 pounds of pure muscle. I guarded him and as I tried to steal the ball, I got caught at a bad angle. He ripped the ball away and I felt agonizing pain in my shoulder. The doctor said I'd torn a muscle, and he put my arm in a sling for a month. Playing was out of the question.

So that was it. I never played again in an official game and my basketball career was over.

Years later Carolynn told me that she thought if I had played pro ball, my weaknesses for women, drugs, and alcohol would have killed me. She believes God spared me. I think she's right.

At the time all I knew was that my body hurt and I couldn't play basketball anymore. I stuffed more disappointment and anger on top of all my other bottled-up feelings. I did what I'd always done with pain: I ran as fast as I could and increased the dose of the painkillers, which for me were not pills but drugs, alcohol, and sex. I hung around the wrong crowd and fed off their attention, which led me to more ruin.

I was in a free fall to certain disaster.

caught

5

I learned that no matter how fast you are, you can't outrun God.

Carolynn surprised me one day in 1992. Without warning she said, "Bill, I'm tired of New York. Let's move to Kentucky. I want to raise Kristen back home." The constant rat race in New York and increasing crime in our north Bronx neighborhood had taken its toll. The city schools were terrible too. Carolynn really wanted a more wholesome environment for our family.

"Yeah. I'm tired of New York too," I said.

What I didn't tell her was that I wanted out of New York because the secret life I was hiding from her was spinning out of control. Maybe in someplace new I could pull myself together.

Carolynn knew I partied, but she didn't know how heavy my drug and alcohol use had become. And for sure she had no clue about my cheating on her. I was a good liar. If I came home late, I told her I had stayed late to catch up at the office. On weekends, my cover story was golf, which was an all-day commitment in New York. Carolynn's a sharp person, but I kept her fooled because I was meticulous about covering my tracks. But as clever as I was, there were times when I was one conversation, one wrong turn, one chance meeting away from getting caught. It reveals something about me that I found this game thrilling.

Even more disgusting was that I blamed Carolynn for my bad behavior. My twisted thinking was, *If she was a better wife and supported me more, I wouldn't have to find something or someone else to please me.* I was selfish and totally focused on me: Billy Rieser had to come first, ahead of everyone else. I thought that if Carolynn ever found out about the other women, she would have a nervous breakdown and kill herself. I was Satan's slave.

Clueless about Marriage

We fought constantly. Poor Kristen heard Daddy and Mommy screaming a lot. I never hit Carolynn, but I landed some knockout blows to the apartment walls. I was clueless about marriage. I thought it was a fifty-fifty deal—"If you do this, I'll do this. If I do this, you should do this." That's a contract, not a covenant. I think a lot of marriages are like that if the couple doesn't put God and His principles first in their relationship. When you can't be honest with yourself and own up to your own failures, you typically pick the ones you love who are close by and take it out on them. That's what I did with Carolynn.

But the messing around and lying and abusing my body—all of it was taking a toll. Besides the addictions, I was piling up debt on bad car deals and gambling. By the time we left New York we owed $40,000.

I liked the idea of running away to Kentucky, because that's how I responded to problems. But God ran right after me. A man I met years later—Max Appel—told me that in life you are either running to the cross of Jesus or away from it. I was definitely hightailing it away from the Lord.

Bingo! ... and Prayer

In a matter of weeks we packed and moved to Lexington. A roommate from college lived there, so I called Scott and asked if we could stay with his family until we found work. We learned there weren't many jobs, so both Carolynn and I ended up in the bingo business helping non-profit organizations raise money. We went all over the state doing this, and I actually became one of the top game callers in Kentucky. There I was, yelling out those bingo phrases with my New York accent: "Luckee sevahn, Gahd's in hevahn . . . Beee sevahn." It was wild and fun, but not so profitable. A good side benefit was that with Carolynn and me together most of the time, I wasn't tempted to cheat on her.

Picking up where she'd left off in New York, Carolynn continued to seek God. She searched for months before finding a great church called Southland Christian Church. She joined several Bible studies, and as she made friends, often asked them to pray for "Bill's salvation." A new senior pastor named Mike Breaux arrived at the church, and the first time Carolynn heard him speak, she concluded that this was one guy I would listen to. She asked me to go but I always found an excuse to stay away. I didn't think there was anything I needed that would be found at a church.

Carolynn's new friends did more than pray for me. Two of the guys asked me to play golf. They were nice, but when they also invited me to church, I shut them off. No way.

Our bingo jobs put food on the table but made no dent in our debt. So when I had a chance to interview with a printing company for a better paying sales position, I jumped at it. The company's first salary offer was low so I turned it down. The owner was not amused and apparently not accustomed to hearing no. He called me in for an interview and yelled and cursed at me: "What the bleep do I have to do to get you to work for me?"

"You didn't offer me enough money," I told him. "But it's not so much the money; it's that I'm in debt, and I've got to make more to pay it off!"

"How much in debt are you?"

We were about forty grand in the red, but I didn't want to admit that, so I told him half: "$20,000."

"Twenty thousand? Here!" He reached in his coat pocket for his checkbook and wrote a check to me for twenty grand. "Can you start Monday?" he growled.

"Sure thing." We shook on it, but as I left I wondered, *Why didn't I tell him forty thousand*?

Same Old Bill

The new job was great for our finances, but the downside was that Carolynn and I no longer worked together. When I got out of her sight, I found new people to get drunk with and women to chase. My old habits resurfaced like a bad carpet stain.

By this time Carolynn had recommitted her life to Jesus and been rebaptized. The more she learned about faith and what a good Christian marriage should look like, the more she wanted my attention and love. But I wanted to play golf and mess around. This caused more arguments. We were going nowhere as a couple.

In the meantime, I took an even better paying sales job in the telecom industry. I was seeing two women, and before long I also got involved with a woman at my office. I was back to my old ways of juggling relationships and hiding them from Carolynn.

My life was out of control again. I could not halt my own self-destruction. I was ruled by my addictions, and the around-the-clock burden of keeping secrets was wearing me out. I was always irritable and restless. This is what sin does when it runs its course. There's some pleasure, but then the bill comes due—and none of us has the resources to pay it.

I liked hitting happy hours at local bars with my female coworkers. This irritated Carolynn, so to quiet her and create a cover for my infidelity, I often invited her to join us. I knew she would refuse to come, so I "cleverly" got her off my back and was able to keep doing what I wanted.

Game Over

I got away with my deceptions until one night in March of 1998 when Carolynn decided to pop into my office unannounced. We had fought about my hanging out at the office late and visiting the bars. This time I was in my cubicle working late. It was about 7 p.m. and the other employees in my area were gone, so I decided I deserved a break from my "hard work." I figured this would be a perfect opportunity to call another woman I wanted to seduce. She answered the phone, and before long our conversation became very intimate.

My view of the outside entrance was blocked, so I didn't know Carolynn had come in and could hear everything I was saying. I didn't know how much of my verbal lust she'd heard, but when she came around the corner and I saw the tears streaming from her eyes, I knew my gig was up. I'd been caught.

Carolynn is mellow much of the time, but this time she went ballistic. She called me every name she could think of. When she stopped yelling to catch a breath, I said, "Do you want to know about everything else? I'll tell you!"

Jerk that I was, and because I was mad, too, I told her about all the other women, even those back in New York. I still felt that in some way this was somehow *her fault*, so I wanted to make her pay! I thought our marriage was dead anyway because I no longer felt any love for her. I'd convinced myself that after a divorce I would begin a new life apart from Carolynn and Kristen. I was being totally selfish and not caring at all about her feelings.

My stories about the other women made Carolynn even more hysterical. She thought she'd known all about my "issues"—the alcohol and drugs, the arrogance, the selfishness, the gambling, the putting myself first over the family. Because she loved me, she'd chosen to put up with all that because there was one thing she could count on: Bill Rieser was "true blue"—he would never cheat on his wife. Now I was crushing her world with a wrecking ball.

As I gave Carolynn the detailed summary of my infidelity, her heart broke. She fell apart in front of my eyes, the sobs shaking her body. And even if I had wanted to comfort her, she would have refused me. Her husband had become her Judas.

We left my office and talked in the car for a couple of hours. After that we went home and talked more. Actually, she did the talking— screaming would be more descriptive. "I trusted you!" she yelled. "How could you?" I had nothing to say. I figured we were history. I saw no way she could forgive me.

Marriage Over?

The first two days or so were horrible because no matter what I said, Carolynn screamed and became hysterical. We hardly ate or slept. Finally, she went to see a pastor for counsel at Southland Christian Church, and he helped her calm down. Carolynn received comfort and was advised that the marriage was not necessarily over. There was a lot of prayer along the lines of "We don't know exactly how Carolynn should respond, but we're going to pray that God will intervene."

I'm so grateful the pastors took that approach because many people—Christian or not—would have said, "Look, Bill was unfaithful to you multiple times. How could you ever trust him? End this bad marriage and move on." I could not have blamed her for doing that, but it would have destroyed our family.

And it might have prevented the miracle that was about to take place.

Our conflict continued day after day. We snapped at each other and had no kind words for each other. Every attempt to talk calmly turned into a screaming fit with Carolynn totally upset. She cried and cried—it was excruciating. I braced for the end.

On a Wednesday night, almost three weeks after I was caught, Carolynn and I had set a time to discuss what we would do next. I assumed this would be the "I'm getting a divorce, Bill" announcement, and we would talk about the logistics of the separation and details of living apart.

Before meeting with me, Carolynn went one more time for prayer with a Southland pastor, Todd Layne. During their time together, Todd didn't say it, but Carolynn read in his eyes his own hopelessness concerning our marriage. But he prayed that in the ordeal Carolynn would have what the Bible promises—a "peace that passes understanding."

At about 7 p.m., Carolynn left the church and started home. She still wasn't sure herself what she wanted to do about us, so she continued praying, "God, I don't know that I can forgive him! I want to but I can't! You are going to have to do something. I can't!" As she drove toward our home on Harrodsburg Road, she prayed again for God's help and "special peace." And He answered.

About halfway to our house, as she was passing Ramsey's Diner, God intercepted Carolynn. She felt the love and peace of God come into the car. His presence overwhelmed her. In an instant she felt God supernaturally taking away the pain and giving Carolynn the ability to forgive me. She felt a peace unlike anything she'd ever felt before. Her heaviness lifted. *Is there hope after all?*, she wondered.

Meanwhile, I was waiting at the house with no clue about what was happening. She had not told me about her appointment with Todd. All I knew was that we were about to have another painful discussion about going our separate ways. When Carolynn stepped through the front door, her appearance shocked me. For the past few weeks, because of all the anger, worry, and fatigue, she had not looked like herself. She came through the door standing straight and with some zip in her step. I even saw a smile on her face. My heart stirred.

"I've Got Something to Say."

I started to ask what was going on, but she interrupted: "Hold on. I've got something to say!" She walked to me and looked me straight in the eye: "Bill, God would never give up on you, and I'm not going to give up on you either. God can forgive you for anything that you've ever done."

She paused. "And so can I!" Tears rolled down her cheeks.

My mind tumbled. For once I had nothing to say.

"I don't know if I can ever forget what you did, Bill, but I'm willing to give it a try if you will give your life to Jesus Christ!" She smiled and continued to stand a few feet away. That's all she said that night. It was all she needed to say.

I felt it—the pull deep inside. God was drawing me. . . . Even before, when Carolynn had spoken to me, I'd known it really was God speaking through her to me. After all my running, and His chasing after me, I was cornered.

I had a choice to make: Go with God or go my own way. In a split second I saw my life played back to me. God showed me all the times He was with me, protecting me, watching over me, loving me. Once again, I saw the rapist in the hallway. I saw the gunmen trying to shoot me during the drug deal. I saw the men following me to the car after the basketball game, the night Jimmy got shot. I saw my slam dunks and the roaring crowds, as well as the day my shoulder tore away and basketball ended.

I saw Carolynn and me standing before Pastor Denvis Rush and saying our vows. I saw Carolynn holding baby Kristen the day she was born.

I saw God there, with me my whole life. And now I had a choice to make.

If I don't do this, I'm going to die. I realized who I was for the first time. I saw my emptiness and futility. I was lost. I sensed Christ was the path to something better, a life I'd wanted but thought I could never have. I wanted to be clean and free and have a fresh start. I told God in my heart, *I'm going Your way. I'll do whatever You want me to do, as long as I know it's You.*

"Yes, I'll accept Christ," I told Carolynn. "And we're going to make this thing work."

satisfied
customer

6

Not everything changed overnight, but I learned that prayer was amazing.

The new Billy Rieser was not like the old one! It was going to take some time for me to get used to the new me.

Instead of "God" being another curse word for me, I *knew* Him personally. I could talk to Him whenever I wanted, 24/7! Quickly, hope replaced my depression. Gone was the likelihood of a nasty divorce, and I was madly in love with my wife again, *fighting* to *save* our marriage! But I knew that just because I felt different did not mean Carolynn could believe me. I had destroyed her trust and had a lot of ground to recover.

After turning my life over to God, one of the first things Carolynn and I sought was professional help. The pastors at Southland Christian Church referred us to a Christian counselor who met with each of us individually and then together. The counseling was helpful, but during our second session as a couple, I got an idea I couldn't shake. I was so young as a Christian that I didn't understand yet about how God communicates with His children. In fact, I was having a strong impression from the Holy Spirit. I blurted to Carolynn, right in the session, "We don't need counseling anymore!" The counselor had proposed at least ten sessions, but I said confidently, "God's healing and restoring us, and we're going to be fine!"

Carolynn was not so sure and gave me a little "yeah, right" look, but I knew I was in love again and would knock myself out to save the relationship. I was overwhelmed by God's goodness and determined not to let Him down. Carolynn was guarded because Satan was constantly tempting her to think that I might still be cheating on her.

Later I told her that we didn't need additional counseling after the two sessions (one individual and one joint session) because I was committed to God, her, and our family. I'm not recommending every couple seeking marriage counseling should go to only one or two sessions; but I sensed we had the basics to get us started on the road back, and now it was time for me, with God's help, to work on my part of loving my wife.

Still, I knew I had to make radical changes in my behavior to convince her that I really had changed. I started going to church with her at Southland and I also quit my job. I knew I would not convince her if I stayed around the people I'd always partied with.

Time to Run Fast after God

Since I'm talkative anyway, I told my story to anyone who would listen, of how God had done a miracle by saving me and rescuing my marriage. I know you can't really practice and excel at being a Christian like you would at playing basketball, but I learned early on that you could be faithful and passionate. Before giving my life to Jesus Christ, I had run in the fast lane and partied hard. It made sense to me to run as fast after God and get as close to "the edge" spiritually as possible.

When I was a baby in my faith, one of my godly mentors, David Jeffares, told me that "if you are fully committed to God and simply believe what the Bible says, God can do more in a two-hour-old Christian than He can in a twenty-year-old Christian." God is looking for *passionate* people, not *perfect* people. He doesn't call the qualified but qualifies the called if we show up and pursue Him with everything we have.

Being passionate for God is what really activates the life of God in us. On the flip side, I see so many Christians living underneath their privileges as a child of God by choosing to "incorporate" God into their lives. God expects more than that! On the cross Jesus paid a steep price for you and me. God will not settle for being an add-on to our busy life. He wants it all. We are asked to surrender our entire life, will, desires, plans, wishes, dreams, and ambitions to Him.

Carolynn's Full Forgiveness

During the time period after I was saved, Carolynn had a job selling decorative patio stones to home centers. This kept her on the road about three weeks a month. On her long drives between sales calls, she prayed for me and our family. In those many hours alone, traveling the long stretches of highway in the Midwest, she listened to Dr. Charles Stanley and others on the radio and slowly processed her feelings and reflected on the changes in our relationship.

She loved me so beautifully and never held me hostage to my past. I know it wasn't easy, but Carolynn made good on her promise to forgive me.

At one point she was agonizing again over the trust issue. She cried out to God, "I know You are doing something great with Bill. But how will I ever be able to trust him again?" The Lord gently replied, *Don't worry about trusting Bill—I'll take care of him. All you have to do is trust Me.* After that the trust torment ceased, and Carolynn was at peace.

A Rookie Believer

Long before I was saved, Carolynn had prayed faithfully for both my salvation and that the Lord would put godly men in my life to walk with me. That prayer was answered even before I became a Christian. As a rookie believer I met a number of solid Christian men at a morning men's prayer group every Tuesday at 7 a.m. at the Springs Inn Hotel in Lexington. Several men led the group, which was linked loosely to the Fellowship of Christian Athletes (FCA) and attended by guys from many churches. The format was simple—breakfast and coffee, a sharing time, and then a good half hour of intense prayer.

I soaked it all in, observing carefully how they conversed with God. Keep in mind that I knew almost nothing about living as a Christian, how I was supposed to talk or act. And I was totally ignorant about the Bible. One day I was telling one of my new Christian buddies about some struggles. He was sobered by my challenges and said, "Man, you sound like Job! You should read the book of Job!" Brilliant one that I was, I went home and asked Carolynn, "Honey, could you buy me this book of Job?"

She gave me a strange look, which happened a lot, so I didn't think much about it. A month later I remembered the conversation and asked her if she'd ever bought that book of Job for me.

"You knucklehead," she said. "It's a book in the Bible!"

Oh. I guess the good thing about my naïveté, though, was that I was like wet concrete that God could shape as He wished. And I was fortunate to be surrounded by people who took the Bible and prayer seriously. These men and women were not insincere when they said, "God said it. I believe it. And that settles the issue."

The men who led the Tuesday breakfast—Max Appel, David Jeffares, and others—expected God to answer prayer. They also believed that God is eager to communicate with us, and during my first Tuesday at this men's gathering, I knew it was God who whispered into my heart, *This is where I want you to be.* OK, that nearly freaked me out, because I was not used to hearing stuff like that! I know now that God often speaks through the Word (the Bible), the wisdom and counsel of godly believers, and at times through circumstances. But He got my attention that first Tuesday by speaking to me through His Holy Spirit, affirming my being with these men each week at 7 a.m.

Another Tuesday morning a new guy showed up. His clothes were wrinkled and it looked like he'd not slept for days. We asked him what was going on and he told us, "I'm addicted to Internet pornography. My wife found out and left me. She says this time it's for good and she's never coming back. My marriage is over. I'm getting a divorce. I heard about you guys. Can you pray for me?"

This kind of thing happened every week, so the men knew what to do. We stood up—probably forty men were present—surrounded the guy, and laid hands on him. All of this was new and a bit bizarre to me, but I went along with it! Some men prayed boldly that this man and his wife would be reconciled; and not just that they would get back together, but that their marriage would demonstrate "God's power and glory"!

Wow, believe me, at first this talking to God as though He were on the other end of a phone line was weird to me, but I also knew what Carolynn's prayers and the prayers of others had done for me, so I was eager to see what might happen.

The next Tuesday this man bounded in with a huge smile on his face. He started talking right away: "I can't explain this, but at 3 a.m. this morning," he said, "my wife came home! She said, 'I don't know why I'm here but God told me to come home. I think we're supposed to work this thing out!'

"It's a miracle!" The guy started to cry, and we all clapped and cheered.

In the months and years that followed, Carolynn and I came to know this man and his wife well. What we had prayed for in the men's group absolutely came true. The couple did work everything out and have a strong Christian marriage to this day.

Our Prayers— Awesome Conversations with God

I know God blessed me incredibly as a young Christian by helping me understand that the Christian life doesn't need to be complicated. Take prayer, for instance. My Christian buddies, at the men's group and at church, taught me that prayer was simply a conversation with God. It was personal and intended to build intimacy between the two of us. Maybe because I'm a relational guy and I like to talk, from the very beginning this personal way of communicating with God made sense to me.

Why do we often make prayer seem weird? Why can't we talk to God like we would to a close friend? And if you haven't spoken to someone for a long time, is it right to expect you will feel close and have a good relationship with that person? The great thing about Jesus is that He is always willing to listen to what we have to say.

My first real prayer turned out to be my best prayer ever—the one I prayed asking Jesus into my life. If you have never done that, you can do it right now and start your own personal relationship with God via prayer. Just do it! Here's a sample prayer you can use:

"Jesus, I believe that You are the Son of God who died for me and my sins. I am asking You to first forgive me of all my sins, and I now accept You as my personal Savior. Please be the Lord of my life from this moment on! I am placing my trust in You alone for the forgiveness of my sins and the free gift of salvation that you purchased for me on the cross."

Once you have asked Jesus into your life as your Savior, you have a relationship with Him and His Father—now your Father—the Creator God. Now you are ready for intimate and awesome conversations with God.

Prayer Is...

It took a few years to come up with this list, but here are some of my favorite truths about prayer:

- Prayer is our connection to heaven and heaven's connection to us—that is why we should always keep the lines open!
- Prayer is as essential to knowing God and growing spiritually as breathing is to living.
- Prayer is a lifestyle, not a thing we do every now and then.
- True prayer is not overcoming God's reluctance, but laying hold of His willingness.
- Prayer is how we let God fight our battles and we get to watch.
- Prayer is how we remind ourselves that we are powerless without God.
- Prayer makes the impossible possible.
- Prayer releases the love and compassion of God to those we pray for.
- Prayer does what you can't do for someone else.
- Prayer tells your problems how big your God is instead of you telling God how big your problems are.

To this day I love talking to God about everything!

Not-So-Happy Hour

For all I was learning about being a Christian, I still had a ways to go. As I said earlier, I didn't know much about how Christians were "supposed" to act. For example, I had no idea what the Bible said about alcohol. A few months after I became a believer in Jesus, some of my friends at work asked me out for a few drinks. I didn't go to bars after work like before, but since Carolynn was in town and could go with me, I said we would come. I would not have done this without Carolynn because I had promised always to let her know what I was doing and to include her in everything. (I still do that. Carolynn knows that she can call me at any time, even when I'm in the middle of a talk to a group, and I'll take the call. I'm always accountable to her because she is everything to me.)

So we went to the bar for happy hour and soon I was very happy: telling jokes, talking about Jesus, and slinging down margaritas. I always had a tremendous capacity for liquor, and apparently even salvation hadn't changed that. Carolynn wasn't drinking but was enjoying herself. After I had whished through about twenty—yes, *twenty*—drinks, I felt a pain in my chest. It scared me—was I having a heart attack? Carolynn and I left the bar and drove directly to an emergency room to have me checked out.

After a battery of tests, the medical team determined that my heart was OK but that I might be experiencing anxiety. The ER doc said, "You need to go see your own physician, because the blood work revealed some things that your doctor should talk to you about."

That's what I did a day or two later. Both Carolynn and I were in the doctor's office when she looked at the test results and told me that the blood work revealed I had hepatitis. And after asking me questions about my past extramarital sexual activity, she said, "I'm worried that you may have the AIDS virus too."

You can imagine how that made me feel. I couldn't look Carolynn in the eye. "We need to do some additional blood work to find out for sure what's wrong," the doctor said, "and it will take seven days to get the results back." A nurse drew blood and we left.

On the way home Carolynn stared ahead, and we didn't talk much. What a blow this health crisis was. Carolynn and I were doing so much better in our marriage, and now this.

Words of Faith

Next Tuesday morning at prayer group I told the men what had happened—all about my drinking too much, going to the hospital, the blood tests, and what my doctor had said. My return visit to the clinic was scheduled later that morning. "I guess I need you guys to pray for me," I said. The whole group gathered around, laid hands on me, and started talking to God. One of the guys was insistent: "Father, we pray for Your healing power for Bill, and that this second set of blood work will not show AIDS or anything serious! We pray this in Jesus' name." While he was praying I felt an unusual sensation in my body. Had God done something?

Later that morning Carolynn and I went to the doctor. While we sat in the waiting room, Carolynn took my hand and, with tears in her eyes, said, "It doesn't matter what the doctor tells us. God's pulled us through so much so far: He's not going to let us down now." *Man!* I was scared, but can you imagine how good it felt to have her say that to me?

We were taken to the doctor's private office where we waited nervously. She was smiling when she came in: "Bill, you had us fooled all week. When the new blood work came in, it revealed that you didn't have AIDS or hepatitis. But there is something wrong with your liver. It's not life-threatening; it's a rare disease called Gilbert's Syndrome, which is triggered by stress and alcohol. It bloats your liver and affects other organs."

I wanted to jump out of my chair and yell "Praise God!" but I restrained myself.

"So here's what you have to do," the doctor went on. "You can't have a drink for the rest of your life, and you must stay happy!"

I was so relieved and excited that I struggled to grasp what had happened. I only knew that we had prayed and now the blood work showed that I didn't have hepatitis or AIDS. I concluded that God answers prayer, even for someone like me!

I had not been a believer in Christ for very long, but already—based on how God was interacting with me and moving in my life and the lives of others—I was a *satisfied customer*.

Carolynn and I both felt that no matter what happened from this point on, we were going to be loyal "customers of God." God had delivered on His promises. Even if He never did another single thing for us, which was unlikely because He is such a giver and loves to be involved with His children, we were sold on Him.

Mountain Mover

Are you aware of the power you have in prayer? As a follower of Christ you can face any difficulty and ask for nothing less than the fullness of God's will for your life. Let's not overcomplicate prayer, but I do believe God desires several qualities in our prayers. First, He wants us to *believe that prayer works*! Here's what Jesus said about the role of faith in prayer:

> "Have faith in God," Jesus answered. "I tell you the truth, if anyone says to this mountain, 'Go, throw yourself into the sea,' and does not doubt in his heart but believes that what he says will happen, it will be done for him. Therefore I tell you, whatever you ask for in prayer, believe that you have received it, and it will be yours." (Mark 11:22–24)

We all have mountains to overcome, things like addictions, bad habits, unforgiveness, fear, selfishness, pride. These are the issues and sins that Jesus says, through prayer, we have the power to order into the sea.

I also believe that God wants us to *pray according to His will*. In 1 John it says: "This is the confidence we have in approaching God: that if we ask anything according to his will, he hears us. And if we know that he hears us—whatever we ask—we know that we have what we asked of him" (1 John 5:14–15).

We are not to pray for whatever we might want—an expensive home, an airplane, a new spouse. We pray for what God wants, and the best way to find that out is to read the Bible. God is not a cosmic Santa Claus or spiritual bellhop. What He wants is for us to represent Him on earth, to ask for ways to touch and help people so they will be reconciled to Him. And we don't have to pester Him all the time to make sure our needs are met. God is generous and has promised to always take care of us.

Relationship Enhancer

Prayer is the engine that activates the life and will of God in our lives. It is not how we *obtain* things but *lay hold* of the things of God for our lives. It is the life breath of communication with God. It is how we draw closer to Him. It is God's number one relationship enhancer tool for us to keep our fellowship with Him growing and strong.

I think too many people come into a relationship with God with the mind-set that if they give their lives to Christ, God will do this and that. And based on what God does or doesn't do, that is their view of God. That's not it! I didn't give my life to Christ thinking that if I did this, God would heal my marriage or do other things for Bill Rieser. I gave my life to Christ because I realized that God loved me, in spite of me, and that I needed a Savior.

Best decision I ever made.

I've never looked back.

Satisfied customer.

a new
peace

7

I learned so much about forgiveness.

orgiven! I was forgiven!

In those first weeks after I said yes to Jesus and let Him take control of my life, I felt so clean! For many years, day after day, the effects of my sin had settled throughout my life like dirty grime that collects on buildings in a city with polluted air. Inside me I had layer upon layer of dirt—cursing God, lying, hating people, cheating on Carolynn, ignoring my daughter, envying the money and lifestyle of pro basketball players, lusting after success. I had about sunk under the weight of all my bitterness and depression.

Basically, I had hated myself. Deep down I'd known I was the one who messed up my basketball career by abusing my body and disobeying coaches. It was my fault my marriage was in shambles.

And then in an instant, a holy God had used the blood Jesus bled on the cross to scrub away my sins and rinse me clean! He had said to me, *Bill, your sins are paid for. I forgive you. You are My son! You can have a fresh start in life. Turn from your sinful ways and do things My way from now on.*

Can you see why I was caught up in the wonder of God's forgiveness? Of course, I had a limited understanding of the meaning of what Jesus said to His disciples about forgiveness: "For if you forgive men when they sin against you, your heavenly Father will also forgive you" (Matthew 6:14). Considering the way I had lived before receiving the gospel, I had many people I needed to forgive. As He always does, in His patient and gentle ways, the Lord would deal with my lack of forgiveness for others—one person in particular—when the time was right.

Intense Thirst

I was so excited about my new life and could not get enough of God! My thirst for knowledge was intense.

Pretty much anytime I had the opportunity to hear a sermon or attend a prayer group, I took it. Now that I knew God personally, I wanted to know everything about His nature and personality. I made appointments with pastors and other Christians and spent hours asking tons of questions: "Why does He love me? What does a relationship with Jesus Christ look like? What does grace mean? What does forgiveness of sins mean? What if I still sin now that I'm a Christian—how does He react to that? Why doesn't God wipe out sinners? How do we know God listens to our prayers?"

Early on I learned something neat about God: When I would ask Him, "Who are You—what are You really like?" He would reveal something about Himself. It was so cool! Before meeting Christ, I was intensely passionate about sports or my sinful habits. Now my passion was directed to God.

Carolynn appreciated my excitement but, understandably, was a little skeptical. She had seen me get wildly enthusiastic about other things, then watched the passion fade. She encouraged me to seek some balance in my life by sticking to the basics—read the Bible, pray, and spend time with godly people. I had to cool my jets a little and be patient, to understand that Carolynn and I were on the same path with God but not at the same mile marker. Above all, I needed to do everything I could to rebuild her trust in me. That was a process and would take time.

We attended several small group Bible studies together. It was great to be able to discuss things with others who had walked with God for decades. And Carolynn's prayer that I would have the right kind of men in my life continued to be answered as a number of guys I met challenged me to grow up as a follower of Jesus, not only by studying the Bible, but by doing what the Bible says. They also encouraged me to be a good husband and father—to serve Carolynn and Kristen by putting their needs before mine. These were all new concepts to me, but I learned to love the truth about life that I found in God's Word.

A Fearless and Bold Model

One of my new friends, Jamie Moore, was fearless in his faith and a seasoned prayer warrior. Some people thought Jamie was too radical, but I loved his "leave it all on the playing field" approach to Christianity. When I met Jamie he was in his late fifties and a veteran of twenty years of prison ministry. Maybe it was the exposure to prisoners all those years, but Jamie was edgy, blunt, and tough. His reckless boldness reminded me of the apostle Peter.

Once he was speaking to a group of murderers awaiting execution. When one of them figured out that Jamie was giving a "religious" talk and sharing the gospel, the prisoner stood up and said, "This isn't for me" and left the room. Later Jamie saw the guy in a hallway on death row and asked, "Why'd you leave? Am I not a good speaker?"

"What you were talking about wasn't for me," the prisoner said.

"What do you mean?"

"You were talking about grace and forgiveness and, you know, having a relationship with Jesus. That ain't for me."

"Why not?"

"You don't understand. I've killed people. That's what I've done."

"Well, how many people have you killed?" The guy was dumbfounded when Jamie asked him that.

"Five or six. I've killed five or six people!"

"Is that all?" Jamie asked.

The prisoner gave him another startled look.

"I know about a guy named Paul in the Bible who killed many people," Jamie went on. "Get this! Not *any* people, but Christians, OK? And God stopped him in his tracks one day and said, 'Stop doing that,' and told him that He loved him. He used Paul to write much of the New Testament.

"I'm not the smartest guy in the world, but if God can forgive Paul for killing scores of Christians, I think He can forgive you for your measly five or six!"

The guy had no good answer for that reasoning and gave his life to Jesus Christ on the spot.

That's Jamie—he believes God desperately wants to rescue, forgive, and help people.

Why the Tears?

Although my life had changed dramatically and I was learning so much about following Christ, I sensed something was missing. There was an uneasiness in me that I could not put my finger on. What was going on?

The summer after my conversion, several guys at Southland Christian Church asked me to go with them to a Promise Keepers men's event in Indianapolis. We loaded into a couple of buses one Friday morning and drove so we could attend the first session that night. We found seats in the Indianapolis RCA Dome, which was filled to the top with boisterous men.

When the worship band began to play, I started to cry. This was unusual because ever since I'd hardened myself on the streets of Harlem, tears had not come easily for me. I sensed the Holy Spirit was working on me, but to do what?

The worship ended and the speaker, Steve Farrar, said almost right away, "Listen, if there's any guy in this place who is dealing with an issue of bitterness or unforgiveness, God wants to use you and give you His peace. God wants you to surrender that stuff to Him tonight, because if you're at odds with another person, you're not going to have God's peace."

Steve went on with his talk, but I was so overwhelmed with emotion that I could not listen. As the tears dripped down my cheeks, I prayed essentially the same prayer as when I'd come to Christ—"God, I'll do anything You want me to do, as long as I know it's You."

What came to mind next was the guy who'd raped me in that brownstone entryway when I was twelve years old. Years earlier, when Carolynn and I were still living in New York, I had caught sight of the man on a street in the Bronx. He was with a woman, presumably his wife, and they were pushing a baby carriage. The rage had erupted in me like a forest fire and I'd wanted to kill him with my bare hands.

Forgiven and Free

Even though Jesus was in my life now and I'd been forgiven of my sins, I had never considered forgiving this man for raping me. All these years later in a football stadium in Indianapolis, I was overwhelmed with *my* guilt for the way I'd held anger in my heart against this man. For the first time I realized that the "rock" representing what he had done to me was not nearly as large as the boulder-sized grudge I held against him. I knew I needed to forgive the man, but before I could do that, I had to ask God to forgive me for holding on to all that bitterness and lust for revenge.

I was able to squeeze out the words, "God, I choose to forgive him, and I release the debt today." Next I heard words coming from my mouth that seemed not mine: "Lord, the same salvation You showed me, I want You to offer that to him, because I want to see him in heaven someday and give him a hug."

As soon as I made that decision to forgive, the tightness inside me loosened, and the emotional wound that had festered all those years was cleansed. Now the ultimate healing could begin. I was free! I felt something I'd never experienced in my whole life—deep *peace*. I received the same peace Carolynn did the night she forgave me, what the Bible calls the "peace that passes all understanding." I was blown away. It felt like a five-hundred-pound bag of cement had lifted off my shoulders. I let it all go, and my general anxiety went with it. The bondage of bitterness was replaced by the freedom of forgiveness.

Walking Out of Prison for Good

We should never underestimate the importance of forgiveness, both its receiving and giving, in our lives. I know it's not easy to forgive. Honestly, if I had not been challenged that night to forgive my rapist, I would not have done it. My feelings toward him, even after I accepted Christ, were tipped more toward hate than love. It didn't matter that all these negative emotions were eating me up and robbing me of peace: I simply did not want to forgive the guy, because I wanted to keep him a prisoner of my anger. But the real prisoner was me. That man had married, had a baby, and gone on with his life. Did he even remember he had committed that crime against me? Did he care about my shame? I doubt it. Or what if he had become a Christian too and was now my brother in Christ? If I had waited for the right feelings toward him, I would never have been able to say, "I forgive him" and receive my own parole and walk out of my jail cell for good.

I agree with Pastor Rick Warren, who has said that one of the biggest lies ever is that "time heals all wounds." In fact, if you don't deal with a wound, time may make it even worse. To be honest, I think I was trying to cut a deal with God: "Please, through Your grace and understanding of my deep wound, let me hang on to this bitterness." God said, "No. I'm sorry too that this happened to you, but you must forgive."

What God has never asked me to do is go find this man and try to achieve reconciliation. Forgiveness and reconciliation are two different things. If God asked me to do it, I would. But He hasn't. What if my coming out of the woodwork and sharing this incident from over thirty years ago caused great pain in the man's family? I will leave all of that to God. If He arranges a reconciliation opportunity, I know the Lord will give me the grace to have such a face-to-face encounter. In the meantime, I have been obedient to God and forgiven the man. And my burden is gone.

Forgive Yourself

One more comment on forgiveness: I run into many people who can accept God's forgiveness, and they are able to forgive another person for even the most horrific sins done to them. Guess who they can't forgive? *Themselves.* Is that a reality in your life too?

If we could meet face-to-face and I learned that you have asked God to forgive you but you still carry a load of guilt, I would look you in the eye and say, "It's not your fault! All that shame and guilt that you carry around with you—that's not your fault. Yes, you did commit sins, but now you are forgiven. Your guilt and shame have been signed over to Jesus. That's what He did on the cross. You can be free now. Go ahead and forgive yourself. If God can forgive you, you can forgive you."

Choose to believe what God has done for you *is* true, and because it is true, you can extend to yourself that same forgiveness and the lifting of that guilt. Choose to make the right decision of faith, and leave the rest to God to work out.

Walk free and be free because Christ has set you free!

Another Faith Step

My Christian friends had asked me when I planned to get baptized. This was another step in my own reconciliation with God. The topic came up one afternoon when I was playing golf at the Players Club in Lexington with a pastor at Southland, Whit Criswall: "Whit, I was baptized as a baby. Do I need to get baptized again?" I asked.

While we were walking between shots, Whit started explaining why I should get baptized again. What Whit said made sense to me. I wanted to get baptized and make a public declaration of my decision to accept Jesus Christ as my Lord and Savior. I knew that baptism wouldn't save me; putting my faith and trust in Jesus Christ had saved me. But baptism was my way of declaring to my family, my friends, and my community that I was saying good-bye to my old life, I was forgiven and clean, and I was going to be resurrected to a new life in Christ Jesus.

Whit told me that baptism was an outward sign of the reality of my unseen, spiritual new life. No way could I say no to that!

Whit baptized me on October 21, 1998, at Southland Christian Church. I had never felt so scrubbed clean. And at peace with God.

a new
identity

8

My life was transformed.

My name was still Bill Rieser, but I had a whole new identity!

What had happened to me is what the apostle Paul told the Corinthians in his second letter, "Therefore, if anyone is in Christ, he is a new creation; the old has gone, the new has come!" (2 Corinthians 5:17).

I've always been an outgoing person, so that part of my personality didn't change. But now instead of talking always about myself and what I was interested in, I could not stop telling people about Jesus.

I had found a good sales job in the telecom industry that required plane travel. I had read that one of my basketball heroes, Pete Maravich, was so on fire for God after he became a Christian that when he got on airline flights, he prayed that everyone on that plane who wasn't already a follower of Christ would get saved!

That kind of boldness turned my crank, so I decided to do something similar every time I took a flight. After coming on board, I would say to God, "Father, I pray for traveling mercies today that You'll protect this entire airplane, the crew, and passengers. And I pray for the salvation of every person on this flight."

One day I entered a plane and sat down next to an elderly couple. They were vibrant, and as we began talking, I could tell they were well educated too. Later, I found they were both college professors.

The three of us talked for about an hour about world events, university education, politics, and other topics, but I didn't mention anything about God. Finally, during a break in the conversation, I prayed silently, *God, do You want me to witness to them? And if You do, please give me a sign.*

Plane Talk about God

The moment after I prayed, the husband asked, "What does FCA stand for?"

I was wearing a vest that had the letters FCA monogrammed inside a cross. "I'm glad you asked," I said, and thought, *Thank You, God.* I knew that was my answer. "FCA is an organization I'm a part of that meets every Tuesday. It's called Fellowship of Christian Athletes, and it's dedicated to introducing Jesus Christ to students in schools across the country. I attend this group because Jesus Christ has changed my life."

"How so?" the lady asked.

"My life was a disaster before I met Jesus Christ. He's healed my marriage, healed me physically—He's blessed me! But those things aren't as important as His saving me for all eternity because of a decision I made to accept Him. That's all I had to do! I decided to accept Him into my life now, and for that I get to spend the rest of my life here, as well as eternity, with Him."

I paused. They were both listening intently. "Oh, and by the way, you guys may not know this, but I've prayed that you would go to heaven!"

"Really?" the man said. "We haven't thought much about heaven."

"Is that right? Let me tell you that before this flight took off, I prayed and asked God that everyone on this flight would be saved, have a relationship with Jesus Christ, and spend eternity in heaven." I knew that God was doing something special because these sophisticated professors were soaking up every word I said.

"If you have ever wondered about how you can spend eternity with God," I went on, "all you have to do is acknowledge that Jesus Christ died on the cross for your sins and believe that He is your Savior." I then quoted Romans 10:9, the verse that says, "If you confess with your mouth, 'Jesus is Lord,' and believe in your heart that God raised him from the dead, you will be saved."

"We'll Do It!"

Before I could say anything else, the lady blurted, "We'll do it!" Her husband nodded in agreement. By now both of them were in tears. She said, "We've never had a spiritual experience like this in our lives."

The plane landed and rolled up to the gate. The bell sounded and people started getting up and pulling bags from the overhead bins. But everyone soon came to a standstill because the cockpit door wouldn't open. The engines were off, so the cabin grew very quiet. The three of us were still seated and the lady asked me, "Can you pray for my husband? He has Parkinson's disease." I had sensed something was wrong—I'd seen the man's hand shaking badly. "Would you pray that God would heal him?" she asked.

"Sure, I'll do that." I remembered the story in the Bible where Jesus asked the man to stretch out a withered hand, so I said to the husband, "Would you give me your hand?" He moved it toward me with great difficulty.

It was quiet on the plane—it reminded me of the hush at certain times during Mass I'd experienced in the Catholic Church. The aisle was jammed with people waiting for the door to open. I wasn't embarrassed about what was happening, but I also didn't want to make a scene. Yet I needed to pray out loud, so in this "holy hush," I started in. And the more I prayed, the more I got "into it." I have a fairly loud voice, so I'm sure many of the passengers heard me earnestly asking for God's love and healing for this man, that the Lord would demonstrate His power and take this sickness away from him. I knew the Holy Spirit was pushing me along, and I prayed like we did at the Tuesday morning prayer group—no holds barred!

When I finished the elderly man was in tears. I probably will never know on earth the extent of healing the man experienced, because I've not seen him again. But I do know that after the prayer he looked at his hand in amazement because it wasn't shaking. I think for the first time in a long time his hand was still. His wife saw this too, and they were both awed by what God had done.

The maintenance people at the airline got the door open, and as I stood to leave, I told the man and his wife, "I'll see you in heaven."

I didn't always have such a dramatic encounter with my seatmates on flights, but time after time, God did bring a curious person to me. And when He gave me the green light, I boldly and joyfully testified about the transformation in my life.

In-Your-Face Christianity

About a year after I gave my life to Christ, Carolynn and I went back to New York City to visit both our family and Times Square Church. Several of my mentors in Lexington had told me about this church and urged me to attend a service. I had never heard of the place, even though while living in New York I once had worked a few blocks away. We arrived at the church, which is at 51st and Broadway in Manhattan, on a Sunday morning. We knew thousands of people went to church there, so we arrived about a half hour early. We were entering the lobby when we heard three Italian guys arguing—they looked and sounded like Vinnie, Tommie, and Louie from my old neighborhood. I got a little upset, actually—*why are these jerks making all this racket in a church*? I was the "new" Bill Rieser and all, but when I got annoyed, I still felt the desire now and then to punch people's lights out.

"Carolynn, you wait here, honey," I said and walked closer to the three guys. I saw that one of them had his Bible open, had his finger in the face of another fellow, and was yelling, "Hey! Right here Jesus said it in Matthew!" I started to laugh—they were arguing about Scripture. I could hardly believe it—in-your-face Christianity! I felt so at home. It reminded me of what I had told some people back in Kentucky who thought I should consider starting a ministry: "What should I call it? 'Get

Saved or We'll Break Your Legs Ministry'"?

A Hug from God

Still smiling, I walked back to Carolynn, took her hand, and said, "Come on, let's go inside and worship. They're just expressing themselves." And right then I felt someone come up behind me and give me a tight hug.

I thought, *This is weird*, because I wasn't expecting to see anyone I knew at Times Square Church. I looked behind me and nobody was there, but I still felt arms around me.

I started to cry, and then I sobbed like a baby, because I knew God was up to something. And I sensed *His* arms around me and *His* love all over me. In my spirit I heard Him say, *I've been here all your life, watching over you, protecting you, loving you, pursuing you, even when you worked right down the street from this church.* And that was true. I had worked at the Sheraton New York Hotel on Seventh Avenue. *I want to welcome you home*, the Lord said.

Then Carolynn put *her* arms around me but did not understand what was happening, because with all the emotion I was feeling, I could not speak. She sensed, though, that God was touching me. When I could talk again, I told her, "God gave me a hug today."

This was the first time ever that I deeply sensed the personal, intimate presence of God the Father. I had been learning about Him and knew He heard and answered my prayers, but I'd never *felt* His love like that.

His touch really sealed the deal for me. I was already radically devoted to God, but now the passion for Him burned even brighter. I would never be the same. I truly was a new person—*in Christ*. And the really great thing is that God wants this new identity for every follower of Jesus, but the Devil will do almost anything to convince you that this is not true. One of his favorite lines is to tell us, "Who do you think you are? You're a loser as a Christian. God may want to do great things with other people, but forget it for *you*!"

Get Rid of the Dead Body

I have met so many Christians who have no idea who they really are because they spend most of their time auditioning for a role in a *Weekend at Bernie's* movies. This 1989 comedy featured two computer guys working at an insurance company who learn someone is stealing from the company. They tell the boss, Bernie Lomax, who invites them to his beach house that weekend to gain the details. When they arrive, Bernie is dead. Larry and Richard, the two computer geeks, figure they may uncover the killer if they take Bernie around as if he is alive—plus they'd like to enjoy a weekend at the beach. The two prop Bernie on the couch and later take him to the beach, where he goes boating and even water-skis. But he's still a corpse.

Similarly, many Christians walk around in their old self, the same self that the apostle Paul said is dead: "I have been crucified with Christ and I no longer live, but Christ lives in me. The life I live in the body, I live by faith in the Son of God, who loved me and gave himself for me" (Galatians 2:20). Apparently even in Paul's day there was confusion about the transformation that occurs when someone is born again. The apostle had to remind several of the churches he wrote to that they needed to stop walking in their dead "Bernie" person and instead walk in Christ, with their new and true identity.

We need to grasp the same concept. Understanding who we are in Christ will always get us back on the right road when we get detoured. One of the many reasons people never change and Christians never experience freedom from addictions, strongholds, or bad habits is that they can never fathom the reality of God changing someone like *them*.

God understood that we would struggle with this, so He goes out of His way to describe us based on Jesus' finished work on the cross. When we want to say we are sinners, God calls us saints! He also uses terms like *holy, redeemed, justified, righteous,* and *sanctified*. Since He's God and made us, He knows the truth about who we really are. We are the ones who struggle to grasp that "reality."

It's a shame, but many—if not most—Christians will spend a lifetime trying to become someone they already are.

All Things Are Possible

I already was flying high spiritually that Sunday morning in New York when I got a hug from God, but the Lord had still another treat in store. The message at Times Square Church that Sunday was given by Pastor Carter Conlon. His topic was "It's Time to Call Off the Party." Pastor Carter retold the story of Samson, leading to Samson's final event, when the Hebrew judge asked God to let him once more have strength to pull down the pillars of the house where the enemy Philistines were celebrating (Judges 16:23–30). Carter made the point that if Samson had asked more of God than to pull down pillars and drop a building on his enemies, who knows what Samson might have received—perhaps even the restoration of his sight? *Samson asked too little.*

Then Pastor Carter spoke about how he imagined the party going on in hell right after Jesus died on the cross. Satan and his crew were celebrating their victory over God's redemptive plan until the third day when a messenger arrived and said, "Hey, boss, it's time to call off the party."

Carter's main point? As followers of Jesus we need to stand against Satan and call off the "party" he's having at our expense. We need to expect far more in our Christian life because of what Jesus finished on the cross.

I took that message deep into my heart. "This is unbelievable!" I whispered to Carolynn. "I've never heard anything like this!" The message had reached into the depths of where God was calling me.

I walked out of Times Square Church as though on a cloud. In one morning I'd had a hug from God and received tremendous confirmation of the truth that with God all things are possible.

That second Christmas after Jesus rocked my world, I received the best present imaginable. On Christmas Eve I was sharing some Scripture with Kristen, then age thirteen. Tears came into her eyes and she said, "Daddy, I used to be so afraid of you."

My jaw dropped. I guess I'd never really known the punishment I had inflicted on her. I didn't know what to say.

"But, Daddy," she went on. "I'm not afraid of you anymore because God has changed your life." Wow—that was the best evidence possible to show what Christ had done. Her words alone made it my best Christmas ever.

Those words of Paul the apostle are true: "You have taken off your old self with its practices and have put on the new self, which is being renewed in knowledge in the image of its Creator" (Colossians 3:9–10).

nothing
held back

9

*There are no limits on
what God can do.*

In my sales job with a telecom firm, I prayed for every appointment and possible deal. My baby Christian prayers were simple: "Lord, here's who I'm calling on today. Will You go before me and grant me favor and bless these conversations and meetings?"

And God opened up the heavens and answered those prayers. Even though I'm an outgoing person, I was not particularly gifted at sales, but I closed deals like a maniac—one of them the largest ever for the company.

I was having a blast. I wasn't bashful about my faith, and with every success that came my way, I gave God credit. I loved the fact that God was walking with me.

As a young Christian the one thing I knew for sure was that I needed to be totally dependent on God and to trust Him completely. And because I didn't "know any better," I prayed for everything, assuming that He was listening and interested in what was happening to me.

I met people where they were at, and as best I could, let God lead the conversations. I've never had a problem talking with strangers, so I constantly told people about what God had done in my life. And when I was asked, "What is it about you?" I told them something about Jesus Christ and my personal relationship with Him.

Carolynn and I felt we were living a life of miracles, as something amazing seemed to occur on a weekly basis, and we grew to expect this. We were not arrogant about this or claiming to be something particularly special to God. But we were trying to hold nothing back related to our faith. "Without faith it is impossible to please God," the Bible says (Hebrews 11:6). I think God was responding to our simple trust in Him and our refusal to impose limits on what He could do.

God Hasn't Changed

I am surprised at how many Christians think that God is not able to do the same things that He did in Bible times because for some reason He does not operate like that anymore. So what are we to make of verses in Scripture that say "I the Lord do not change" (Malachi 3:6) or "Jesus Christ is the same yesterday and today and forever" (Hebrews 13:8)? I see no evidence in Scripture to support the idea that God is not as active in the lives of people as He ever was. God remains present in the person of the Holy Spirit dwelling in each believer, just as during the days of the early church. God is active!

I do not mean that God is like a giant bellhop in the sky, always on call to do whatever we want Him to do. He is God and I'm not, so I can't explain His every move. But I wonder—is it possible that what has changed is our perception of who God is and our ability to lay hold of what He has promised? That's worth some thought and prayer.

"Radical" Prayer

I had met some folks who got together for intercessory prayer on Tuesday nights. They had invited Carolynn and me to join them, but since they had the reputation for being radical in how they approached God, we didn't know what to do. In fact, this group seemed a little weird to me. These people were over the top for God—you never could quite predict what they might say or ask you to do in the area of prayer or obeying God. I've since discovered that more of us need to go out to "the edge" in trusting God—He loves to use people like that. But at this point in my journey, I didn't know what to think.

One of the guys in this intercessory prayer group was persistent, so I finally agreed to attend. I asked Carolynn if she wanted to come along but she declined. She did encourage me to go and gave me an urgent request: "Would you ask them to pray for Charlotte?"

Charlotte, who was Carolynn's best friend, had recently been diagnosed with an advanced—level four—brain tumor. Emergency surgery was scheduled for later that week on Friday, but the doctors were not giving her much hope for long-term survival.

"OK, I'll go and ask for prayer for Charlotte," I said.

A little nervous, I showed up for the meeting at a room in Southland Church. There were about ten people there, all intense and eager to head for the "throne room of God." Before the prayer started, I told them about Charlotte. "Would you pray that God would heal her?" I asked. No problem for this group. They gathered around, laid hands on me, and began to intercede for Charlotte.

While they were praying, a picture popped up in my brain. I saw Charlotte in a fire and some hands (I took them to be God's) pulling her out of the flames.

If that wasn't enough, my friend Jamie Moore—right in the middle of his prayer—suddenly blurted out, "Whoa! God told me just now that Charlotte's been healed. He's healed her of this cancer. But she's going to die of a broken heart, not of cancer. And God's not going to heal her of her broken heart. I don't know what that means."

This nearly flipped me out. I had seen this neat picture in my head of God pulling Charlotte out of a fire, and now Jamie had said that God had healed Charlotte but she was going to die anyway? This was getting crazy! After the prayer ended, I asked Jamie, "What am I supposed to think about what you said?"

He didn't have an answer. Jamie knew nothing about Charlotte or her life, other than what I had said about her brain tumor.

Radical Answer

I found out later that while I was still praying at the group, Charlotte had called Carolynn and said, "Something strange is happening to me tonight."

"What do you mean?" Carolynn asked.

"Do you know if there's anybody praying for me?"

"It's funny that you ask, but Billy went to an intercessory prayer meeting tonight and I asked that they pray for you."

"Well, about fifteen minutes ago, I felt like my feet were lifted up off the ground. I felt like God touched me tonight."

When I came home later Carolynn told me about Charlotte's call, and I told her what Jamie had said. Carolynn was skeptical—she thought Jamie was kind of out there on the spiritual lunatic fringe anyway.

On Friday Charlotte went in for surgery, and the doctors found that her brain tumor had shrunk in half since her scan a week earlier. They removed the tumor and sewed her up.

Charlotte was thrilled and recovered. About four months later, though, her husband—a man she totally adored—told her he was leaving their marriage. She was heartbroken.

Several years passed, and Charlotte developed another serious tumor. When this happened, she told Carolynn, "I wish God would have let me die during that first surgery." She had never recovered from the sadness of losing the love of her life. She died six months later.

As odd as it seemed, what Jamie had said that night came to pass. At that "strange" intercessory prayer group meeting, I had experienced something supernatural, an event that helped solidify my understanding of God and His ways. I was more convinced than ever that God was very much alive and active in the affairs of the earth He'd created.

Of course, Carolynn and I know God does not always operate this way in healing situations, nor does God always heal. Pain and suffering and even death can be used for His glory just as well as a complete healing. But when God chooses to, He can move in very powerful ways.

We have also come to realize that healing is a subject that will never fully be understood or answered this side of heaven. One out of every one will die, and many of those deaths will be from ordinary illnesses, just as people in the Bible died from illnesses. I have learned to pray—and pray in faith—trusting that the final outcome will come from God's hand, and with that I can have peace in that situation.

Should I Tell My Story?

I had been meeting now and then with Mike Breaux, our pastor at Southland Christian Church, and he must have seen deeper growth in me because in February of 2000, he asked me to give my testimony during all six of the weekend services at the church.

"Thanks, Mike, but I don't have a testimony."

"No, I want you to do this. You're the most excited person here. You're evangelizing everywhere and bringing people to church. Some are getting saved and baptized. You've definitely got a story."

I told him I would pray about it. I went home and asked Carolynn what she thought.

"What? You don't have a testimony!" she said. "What are you going to say?"

I think Carolynn's lack of enthusiasm related to the fact that much of my story was not flattering. Did we want the whole church to know about my unfaithfulness, for example?

"I don't know what I'll say!" I said.

"You'd better write it down," Carolynn advised.

"I don't know if I can do that. I've never written my story."

"You'd better. You know the sermons are thirty minutes. You can't go over or go less."

I started writing, but the words seemed stuck. I could not get more than about two sentences on paper before I stalled. I was frustrated and I whined to Carolynn about how hard it was. She and I got into some really good fights about the whole deal.

"You're not ready to do this!" she said.

"Honey, I feel that God wants to tell me what to say when I get up there. I can't explain it, but I don't know what my testimony is. I can go back and think about certain events, but I can't write it down for some reason."

A Spiritual Battle Brews

"Well, you're going to blow it," she concluded, and we had another big argument. I didn't know this back then, but I've since learned that sometimes this is how Satan shuts us down. An innocent comment can do the trick and you lose your courage.

I still was not sure, though, what I should do. I mentioned my dilemma to my intercessory prayer buddies. By this time I had joined several prayer groups and at the first one, when I mentioned the invitation from Mike Breaux, they all gathered around me and started praying. At the end of the prayer time a lady said, "I felt impressed—I believe it's a thought from God—I don't know what your testimony is, but there's a war going on right now in the spiritual world for your life. God wants to show you He's winning the battle for you. I don't know how He will show you, but He will."

Whoa—kind of spooky! I thought.

"Satan doesn't want you to give this testimony," the lady continued, "and he's going to do everything he can to discourage you, because I think thousands of people are going to hear this message and get set free and give their lives to Christ."

I didn't know what to say. Sometimes people say things like this but you wonder, *God, is that You*? Sometimes it's another voice from the other side. I thanked the lady but decided to wait for more confirmation.

About a week later another prayer group prayed for me about giving my testimony and a guy there said, "There's a battle going on for your life right now." *Hmmm.* "Satan doesn't want you to give this testimony because thousands of lives are going to be changed. They're going to be set free and they're going to give their lives to Christ."

Wow. "I don't know where this came from," he went on, "but I feel like God wants to show you that He's got this battle won for you. He's taken care of this for you."

How crazy was this! On the next Tuesday, only four days before the Saturday that I was going to speak in church the first time, my regular team of Tuesday night intercessors prayed for me, and when we were done David Jeffares blurted out, "There's a battle going on for your life! Do you know that, Bill?"

"I know now, because you're the third person who's told me!"

"God wants to show you that He's winning the fight for you. I don't know how He's going to do that, but He will. And Satan doesn't want you to give this testimony. There's a major battle going on, but God wants to show you that He's taking care of the fight for you."

A Powerful Answer

A night or two later I was sound asleep in our bedroom, which was next to our front porch, when at 4 a.m. I was awakened by a massive thunder and lightning storm. The thunder was booming nearby, shaking the house, and I saw one lightning bolt after another. Then the rain came, in great sheets, with such force that I was afraid there might be a flood. I shut the windows and tried to sleep, but I couldn't. I wondered why Carolynn didn't wake up.

The storm finally broke and when I didn't hear the sound of raindrops on the roof anymore, I decided to go outside and check out any damage. The sun was rising and when I stepped on the porch, I was puzzled. There was no sign of a rainstorm. I looked along the street curbs and only found dust and pieces of trash. I reached down and rubbed my fingers through the grass on my lawn: dry as a bone. *What's going on here?* I looked up at the sky—not a cloud in sight.

I went back onto the porch, scratching my head. I sat down and that's when the Lord spoke to me—a deep impression in my spirit: *This is the sign David and the others spoke of. I am winning this battle for you. I wanted you to see this sign. Go and speak. I'll give you what you need to say. I love you.*

I cannot tell you exactly how God accomplished this unusual fullblown thunderstorm that came and went without a trace. What I do know is that a shaky young believer learned that God is willing to pull out all the stops to spread the gospel and is able to give direction and peace during spiritual battles.

Again, I'm not saying that God always uses the spectacular to confirm His love. But the 4 a.m. storm was a powerful reminder that He always has His eyes on us and will defend us when necessary.

That weekend I spoke six times at all the services. I spoke boldly without notes. I didn't go over or under the allotted time. I have given my testimony many times since then, always without notes. (By the way, this book represents the first time I've actually put my entire testimony on paper, and a friend is helping me with the writing!)

When Carolynn woke up that morning after the storm, I asked her if she'd heard the thunder during the night.

"No, was there a storm?" she asked, yawning like a contented cat.

the word

10

I love the Bible because it is all about God.

I'd been told that the Bible had the answers to all my questions, so not long after coming to Christ I rushed out and bought a Bible. My first one was called *The Journey Bible*—that was perfect for me because I was on a wild journey!

When it came to the Bible and learning more about God, I was like a kid in a candy shop. I carried my Bible everywhere and read it every spare minute. When I heard something new, I would often ask, "Where is that in the Bible? I want to write that down."

I took the Bible straight up: "If this is what it says, I believe it." I went after God as hard as I went after anything in my life, basketball and golf included. I became "a student of the game."

I can't take any credit for this, but almost from the day my heart was turned toward God, I found it easy to remember Scripture. I wasn't able always to quote a verse word for word and I might foul up the exact references, but when I needed to remember something, I had a nearly uncanny ability to recall the words. Of course this was the Holy Spirit working in me, but back then I had no idea what was going on! For sure it wasn't some forgotten aptitude, because I had not been known for my memory in school, for example.

How Bizarre This Was!

Not long after my salvation Carolynn and I were meeting with a friend who was going through a difficult circumstance. She told us about problems in a relationship, and it was obvious she was really upset and anxious. We listened to her pour out her troubles and in the middle of the conversation I said, "I heard a Scripture that I know will help you. Do you know that Philippians 4:6 and 7 says, 'Do not be anxious about anything, but in everything, by prayer and petition, with thanksgiving, present your requests to God'? And if you pray like that you will experience the 'peace of God, which transcends all understanding.'"

Carolynn gave me a puzzled look and said, "Where did you get that?"

"I don't know!" And honestly I could not tell her. I knew I had read or heard the verses somewhere and retained them.

I even pulled verses from the Old Testament, which I know is a little unusual for a new Christian! One time I was talking to a friend about unity and I said, "Well, Amos 3:3 says, 'Can two walk together unless they are agreed?'" You would have to know me personally to realize how bizarre this was! After all, I was a punk from Harlem who'd grown up on the streets. Quoting anything from memory, other than statistics on the New York Knicks, had never happened before!

How Dynamic His Word

I also saw how dynamic God's Word is—it truly is as Hebrews 4:12 states, "The word of God is living and active. Sharper than any double-edged sword, it penetrates even to dividing soul and spirit, joints and marrow; it judges the thoughts and attitudes of the heart."

One night after completing a business trip in Houston, I boarded a flight to Dallas. Several of us from my office were traveling together, and our plane did not leave until 11 p.m. I was bone tired but after finding my seat, I decided to read a section or two from a devotional book I often carry, *Strong in the Lord*. This little book is a collection of warfare and protection-type prayers. It also has Bible selections, and as I settled into my seat, I was prompted to look at Psalm 91 and meditate on verse 4— how God will "cover you with His feathers, and under His wings you shall take refuge; His truth shall be your shield and buckler" (NKJV).

I put the book down and meditated on those words, which seemed on fire in my mind. A lady next to me in the window seat started a conversation. I made a joke. "You need to know I get very sick on flights so if you have an extra barf bag, could I borrow it? I'll give it back." She laughed.

The plane left the gate and headed down the runway. As the wheels lifted from the ground, I looked out the window and saw one of the plane's tires blow out. A big piece of rubber flew up and was sucked right into the engine intake and, in an instant, flames and black smoke poured from the engine.

By this time we were about fifty feet above the ground, and with the plane shaking and groaning, I could tell we were struggling to gain altitude. The plane was straying off course, and it seemed the lone engine might stall at any time. Some passengers started to scream—it was chilling to hear such fear.

The lady next to me yelled out, "Jesus, save us!" I realized why God had directed my attention to verse 4 of Psalm 91, and after the lady screamed, I took my little book and pointed to the verse and yelled above the bedlam, "See that? Read that." And she looked at it quickly and said, "It's going to be all right, isn't it?"

"It is," I said. I started praying softly, and she did too. The plane was shaking and twisting, the engine roaring and choking, but in a blink we felt a fresh surge of power, and the plane began to gain altitude.

I never found out exactly what happened, but it seemed like an auxiliary engine had kicked in. We climbed some, to a thousand feet or so, and then we circled and came straight back down onto the runway. We bumped hard as we landed, but that was it—nobody got hurt.

The whole thing happened so fast—I estimate about five minutes— that the pilot or a flight attendant never said a word. When we got off, the damaged engine was still smoking.

I said good-bye to my seatmate, and called Carolynn to tell her how God had taken care of us, as He had promised in Psalm 91. I recognized how important God's Word is in revealing truth and reminding me of His faithfulness on normal days, as well as on the day your airplane is struggling to stay aloft.

How True His Word

One of my new friends explained to me the importance of the mind in my walk with God, and how I needed to see the Bible as a source for the right things to think about. My mind needed to be "renewed," and when I had any thoughts that were not lining up with God's ways, I needed to take those "captive": "We demolish arguments and every pretension that sets itself up against the knowledge of God, and we take captive every thought to make it obedient to Christ" (2 Corinthians 10:5).

Even I knew that thoughts involving lust or revenge were wrong, but what about all the other stuff that flows through our minds? I learned that the reliable way to consistently evaluate the quality of my thought life was to have a standard to measure against. Of course the Bible is that standard because every word in that Book is true. By knowing the Word of God, I could distinguish if the source of a thought was God or Satan. Every lie of the Enemy is countered by a truth of God.

Here are a few examples of an Enemy lie that is exposed by one of God's truths:

- The Enemy says you are trapped in chaos; God says you can have peace. "For God is not a God of disorder but of peace" (1 Corinthians 14:33).
- The Enemy says the economy will ruin you; God says your needs will be met. "And my God will meet all your needs according to his glorious riches in Christ Jesus" (Philippians 4:19).
- The Enemy says God could not possibly love you; God says His love never falters. "Let them give thanks to the Lord for his unfailing love and his wonderful deeds for men" (Psalm 107:8).

- The Enemy says you are incapable of dealing with a particular situation and tries to instill fear in you; God says He "has not given us a spirit of fear, but of power and of love and of a sound mind" (2 Timothy 1:1:7 NKJV).
- The Enemy says, "You have no future"; God says, "I have a plan for your future." The book of Proverbs declares with confidence: "There is surely a future hope for you, and your hope will not be cut off" (Proverbs 23:18).
- The Enemy says, "Despair!" God says "Have joy!" That's why King David could write, "You have made known to me the path of life; you will fill me with joy in your presence, with eternal pleasures at your right hand" (Psalm 16:11).

Don't let Satan push you around with his lies! I remind you: As vital as it is to believe that there's a God who loves you, it's as vital to believe there's a devil who hates you. Satan has a plan for your life—and it's not good (see John 10:10).

On a Grand Adventure

I was so curious about everything related to God's Word that I was not afraid to ask questions. One time I was in a Bible study and a woman started talking about "pulling down strongholds."

"What are you talking about?" I asked.

She knew Scripture well and replied, "Well, the 'weapons of our warfare are not carnal but mighty in God for pulling down strongholds'" (2 Corinthians 10:4 NKJV). She could tell from my blank look that there was a problem of communication. She went on to explain that a "stronghold" was anything in your life that is not of God, where deceiving sin has taken hold. It can be an addiction, a problem with anger, lust—whatever.

"OK, I understand, but how do you do that? How do you pull down a stronghold?"

She went on to explain that everything ties back into God's truth. If we know His Word, then we can identify what is deception. And when we identify what is wrong (that is, a stronghold), then we can come against it with prayer and God's power. We can simply say, "God, this is Your truth in this situation. You take care of this. You take this away. I mean, You crush it; You defeat it." And so God takes care of it for us.

After that, I really fell in love with the Bible. No doubt, there was much in the Book I didn't understand, but to me it was a grand adventure to open those pages and find out what God was like and how He relates to people—to grasp more and more how much He loved me.

Not long after I accepted Christ, I read a book by Jim Cymbala entitled *Fresh Wind, Fresh Fire.* Jim is the pastor of the Brooklyn Tabernacle, a New York City church about a thirty-minute weekend drive from where I grew up. In his book, Jim explained how there's so much to learn from the many prayers in Scripture. I sensed God saying to me, *I want you to study all the Bible's prayers, because there are reasons why I answer those prayers.*

The Bible on Prayer

That was all the encouragement I needed. "God," I said, "I want You to show me how the Bible is a book of prayer. Show me every prayer that's ever been prayed in this Book. Show me what was in that prayer, how You answered that prayer, why You answered that prayer, and how I can apply that to my life."

The Bible came alive during that study on prayer. Even familiar sections on prayer, like Jeremiah 29:11—"'For I know the plans I have for you,' declares the Lord, 'plans to prosper you and not to harm you, plans to give you hope and a future'"—yielded rich insights. I knew that many Christians read that and concluded, "Well, cool, God has a great plan for me. It's not a plan for disaster, but it's a plan to give me a future and a hope. I like that."

What they may not realize is that there's only one way to get that plan, which is revealed in the verses that follow. This promise of God's in Jeremiah is basically what He would like to do for every single person who puts faith and trust in Him. But the Lord goes on to say that "then you will call upon me." That means the key to making the plan work is— you guessed it—to *pray.*

Christians often make the mistake of thinking that God's going to do something because He's God. He doesn't operate that way. God responds to the things that we ask Him for: He waits for us to ask Him. God wants to fulfill His promises to us, but we have to ask. (James wrote, "You do not have, because you do not ask God" [4:2].) Of course, God is not limited, so He can and may act without our asking—or asking in doubt instead of faith. But it's clear God wants us to ask so He may bless and increase our faith.

In Jeremiah 29 we also see how to pray: "You will . . . find me when you seek me with all your heart" (v. 13). This is how we get the plan with "hope and a future" (v. 11)—when we pray and earnestly seek Him with our whole heart. In other words, a person who is casual in seeking God will never know God's plan. The person who comes to church on Sunday but puts God on pause on Monday is not seeking after God.

I learned similar insights over and over as I carefully studied prayers in the Bible. And if a particular Scripture was not a prayer, I took what was there and made it into a prayer.

The Perfect Book

More recently in my Bible reading, God has shown me how often there's a progression of events in God's Word—"if you do this, here's what will happen." For instance, 1 Peter 5:5 says, "God resists the proud, but gives grace to the humble" (NKJV). The very next word after that is "therefore." In other words, here comes an action item. If God opposes the proud but gives grace to the humble, let's be sure we know how to be humble. I don't need God opposing me! I want Him on my side, not against me.

The instructions are clear: "Therefore, humble yourselves under the mighty hand of God." And then God throws in a great promise: "that He may exalt you in due time" (v. 6 NKJV). Many of us get tripped up because we want "due time" to be right now. We need to be patient. God doesn't back out of His promises. Due time will come "due."

Similarly, Romans 12:2–3 instructs us that if we no longer conform to the pattern of this world but instead are "transformed by the renewing of [our minds]," we "will be able to test and approve what God's will is." So by leaving the world's pattern and renewing our minds, we can experience transformation and know God's good, pleasing, and perfect will.

If you haven't done so already, I encourage you to fall in love with God's Word. I am convinced that Satan will use almost any trick to keep us away from the Bible. Don't let him get away with it. As a child of God you have been given a "manual" for life that contains all the relevant instructions.

The Book is also a love letter from God to you. I urge you to see study of the Bible not as a religious chore but rather as the reading of the *one* Book that tells the truth about God, His character, and His ways— *perfectly.*

promptings
11

The Holy Spirit became my guide.

After reading Jim Cymbala's *Fresh Wind, Fresh Fire*, I had to check out the Brooklyn Tabernacle. I knew this church had a strong emphasis on prayer and God was moving there in remarkable ways, so I wanted to visit at my first opportunity.

About a year after I was saved, David Hysong (one of my prayer partners) and I were able to visit New York and attend the Brooklyn Tabernacle Tuesday night prayer service. We arrived at the church early, which was good because I learned that if you didn't show up an hour before the prayer meeting began, you wouldn't have a seat. At the time, about two thousand people came and packed out the house. Those who arrived late stayed outside and prayed on the street.

"Don't Ask God for Anything."

At the beginning a fellow got up and said, "If you're a guy, come forward—we want all the men up front." (I didn't know it until my first visit, but the leaders do not set an agenda in order to allow the Holy Spirit to move at these meetings. Tonight, it began this way.)

David and I joined hundreds of men in the aisles. When we got to the altar, the pastor said, "While you are up here, I want you to do a couple of things, but the most important is that I don't want you to ask God for anything."

Whoa, whoa, whoa! I thought. *I came here to pray*! Before I'd left Lexington I was so excited about this prayer meeting that I had collected prayer requests from many people. I was a little naïve—I thought I could show up at the "famous" Brooklyn Tabernacle Tuesday night prayer meeting and—*boom*—get a bunch of prayers answered. I was disappointed with the way the meeting was going.

"What I want you to do is thank God for anything and everything you can possibly thank Him for and praise Him for who He is," the pastor said, and the men around me rumbled, "Amen!" He went on: "And spend the first portion of this meeting doing that, but please specifically do not ask God for anything."

I calmed my expectations and mumbled, "OK, I can do that." All the men started to pray individually but speaking out loud, thanking and praising God. I began by praising God for who He is and thanking Him for healing my marriage, thanking Him for Carolynn, thanking Him for Kristen, thanking Him for healing me, thanking Him for all my blessings.

I took a breath and glanced at my watch—about five minutes had passed. So I dug in and started praising Him for other great, but maybe less spectacular things He had done. I did my best, but it seemed as though this prayer time was going on and on and on.

Praising God for Everything

After about a half hour, during which I had thanked God for everything from paved streets to toothpaste, I sputtered out of gas and my mind started going blank. But the Lord renewed my energy, and I started praising and thanking Him at a deeper level. I realized something interesting was happening: By now the time had stretched to over an hour, and gradually, during this whole experience, the volume of praising and adoration had grown louder and louder. And the men up front were not the only ones praying—every person in the auditorium was doing the same thing. This great roar of prayer was deafening, and all of it was praise and thanksgiving! As a mass, unified body we were declaring to our King how great He is!

The mood was so spiritually electrifying that I had goose bumps. The people around me were crying out from the deepest parts of their soul, thanking God with all their might. I could tell that many of the men were fresh off the streets. I heard guys saying, "Thank You for saving my life!" "Don't let me go back to doing heroin again!" "Thank You for setting me free!"

We reached a peak of praise where it seemed as if God said, "I must respond to this!" and eagerly made His presence known. Scripture says that where two or three are gathered in His name, God is there too (see Matthew 18:20). So of course He was already present in the meeting, but it was like He wanted everyone to know it, because in a split second, the entire group of several thousand people spontaneously burst into song. No one got up and said, "Let's all sing such and such song." It just happened. I was astounded.

The singing continued for about twenty minutes, one song after another, great enthusiastic, loud worship.

When the worship subsided, Pastor Cymbala stood and talked for a few minutes, and then everyone broke into small groups and started praying again. Cards with prayer requests were passed out and we prayed over those. And I did get an opportunity to share the prayer list I'd brought with me, although that didn't seem quite so important anymore.

Finding a Cab

The prayer meeting ended at about 10 p.m., and David and I had to find a way back to our hotel in Manhattan. This part of Brooklyn was so crime-ridden that I knew no cabbie would come so late to pick us up. Growing up in New York I had made a rule: I would ride a subway until 9 p.m., but after that, I always took a cab. Finding a cab would be the problem.

Outside the church, David asked, "How are we getting out of here?"

"We need to find a cab."

"How do we do that?"

"Why don't we pray for one?" I said, "Father, I pray in Jesus' name that You'll get a cab for us."

I felt the Holy Spirit nudging me to walk across the street, so we crossed over, and at that moment, a yellow cab pulled around the corner and stopped: "Are you guys going to the city?" the driver asked. I noticed when we got in that there was an open Bible on his dashboard. The driver turned around and asked, "Would you mind if I play Christian music?"

David smiled at me and said, "God dispatched a cab driver for us, huh?"

The perfect ending to my first experience at the Brooklyn Tabernacle!

That evening at the Brooklyn Tabernacle expanded my understanding of the purpose of prayer: God was more interested in my worship than my prayer list. A verse in Hebrews describes this well: "Through Jesus, therefore, let us continually offer to God a sacrifice of praise—the fruit of lips that confess his name" (13:15). I realized how important praise and thanksgiving are as a prelude to intercessory prayer, and from that night until now, I always seek to praise and bless God before discussing my requests. I know He wants me to bring my list, but He wants to hear how much I love Him too.

The Forgotten One?

I also developed a new appreciation for the role of the Holy Spirit in guiding both public worship and private actions. Jesus described the Holy Spirit as a Counselor, Comforter, or Helper (see various versions of John 14:26). In my brief journey as a new believer, I had learned that the Holy Spirit is the most controversial member of the Trinity. Actually, I think the Holy Spirit has gotten a bad rap! He is, as you know, *God* living in us but too often He seems "The Forgotten One."

In many churches in America today, I believe the two least-spoken-about subjects are prayer and the Holy Spirit. No doubt some weird things have happened when individuals or groups have distorted the work of the Holy Spirit, which has made many Christians fear the Holy

Spirit! What a strange turn of events after Jesus told His disciples that it was for their *good* that Jesus would go to heaven so the Counselor (Holy Spirit) could come (John 16:7). It should never be weird to be full of and walking with the Holy Spirit! Yet, many Christians, wanting not to be "weird"—and who would blame them?—avoid the Holy Spirit.

My advice in regard to evaluating unusual spiritual events or behavior is to test them as the Bereans did. The Bereaans were the New Testament believers who carefully compared what Paul taught with what Scripture said (Acts 17:11). Any time a teaching did not agree with the Bible, the Bible won. It wasn't that they didn't believe, but they wanted to make sure they clearly understood God's desires. Literally, because of all the persecution, their lives were on the line. If they had to die, they wanted to make that sacrifice for truth.

Early in my walk with God, He started testing me with promptings to see how obedient I would be. We cannot ignore the fact that the Bible says it is impossible to please God without faith (Hebrews 11:6). Listening to the Spirit and responding obediently involves faith. That pleases God.

The arguments about the Holy Spirit saddens me. Rather than have strife, we need to be thankful that Jesus sent us the Counselor to guide us into "all truth" (John 16:13). What an honor to have the Holy Spirit living in us, constantly coaching and comforting us!

I think balance is the key to keeping all of God's life flowing through us so that we can be used by Him. God is looking for good representation. If our fruit is ripe, we get to represent Him in His fullness. If our fruit is bad, we become poor examples of who He is. The expression "God is looking for good fruit and not religious nuts" is what has motivated me to seek a life of balance.

Balance is the combination of operating in great faith but trusting the Holy Spirit to lead and guide you in everything you do. It is also letting the Word of God be your check-and-balance system for evaluating what you encounter. In *Fresh Wind, Fresh Fire* Jim Cymbala quoted the old saying, "If you have only the Word, you dry up. If you have only the Spirit, you blow up. But if you have both, you grow up."

That makes a lot of sense to me!

A Boy Alone in Maysville

Personal guidance from the Holy Spirit is a great privilege. It also can be convicting.

After I shared my testimony at Southland Church, I started getting invitations for speaking engagements. Many of them were set up through FCA for school groups, and one of them was for a Valentine's Day event for a middle school group in Maysville, Kentucky.

I enjoyed the hour drive from Lexington and arrived early at about 5:30 p.m. I liked having some extra time to check the place out and pray. I headed into the school and sat down on a bench outside the banquet meeting room. I had my Bible out and was appreciating a few quiet minutes.

The kids started drifting in, and I noticed one boy come in by himself. God immediately drew my attention to him, and it was as though I could see the state of the kid's heart. It wasn't good. He looked sad, and it seemed like it took him five minutes to walk by me. As he passed by, a thought popped into my mind: *Go over to him and share Psalm 34, verse 18.* That verse says, "The Lord is close to the brokenhearted; he rescues those whose spirits are crushed" (NLT).

I had a quick answer for the Lord: *God, my answer is no. I'm not that type of Christian. I don't do this kind of weird stuff*! In my defense, I'd never been prompted before by the Holy Spirit to do anything quite like that. *What's the deal with a specific verse?* I wondered. But the Lord wants obedience, which I was about to learn.

Go over and tell him that. Share Psalm 34, verse 18, and tell him that I love him.

What was the matter—wasn't God listening to me? So I repeated my answer, *No, I'm not going to do that.* In my mind I was here in Maysville to deliver my testimony and maybe see some kids accept Christ. I needed to prepare spiritually for my talk; I didn't have time for this unplanned errand.

A Wrestling Match

But the Holy Spirit did not let up, so I wrestled with Him. The boy had seated himself on a bench in the hallway, and as the other kids came in, no one said a word to him. He seemed alone.

Ten minutes passed. The request was repeated by the Lord. My answer was the same. Ten more minutes—same scenario.

My hosts arrived and we moved to the banquet room, and after I got settled at the head table, I saw that this boy was sitting at a table all by himself. The Holy Spirit went at me again: *Go share Psalm 34:18 with him and tell him I love him.*

No!

I struck up a conversation with the pastor and his wife near me. They had set up this FCA dinner. We introduced ourselves and started talking "shop" about God—"The Lord's doing this and God's doing this, He's great. . . . " Honestly, it was baloney, because by now the Lord was all but twisting my arm and saying, *Go over there and share Psalm 34:18 and tell him I love him! That's all I want you to do!* He was so insistent that I could hardly concentrate on what I was hearing from the others at our table.

Now, in the middle of this conversation, I looked around the room and each of the big round tables had about ten boys and girls, and there was this kid—the one God was pointing out to me—sitting at a table all by himself with his head down.

Meltdown in Maysville

It was now about fifteen minutes before I was scheduled to speak. We were finishing our meal, but the food was sticking in my throat because I was disobeying God. And I knew He was getting impatient with me.

I was still talking to others around me and playing the role of "distinguished guest speaker" when out of the blue I started weeping like a baby. I was a mess—the tears were flying out of my eyes. This was totally out of character for me; it was a God thing. The people at the table became concerned. Was I having a nervous breakdown? Was I about to have an epileptic fit?

Once more I sensed God speaking. This time it was a word of warning. *If you don't go up and tell the boy that Scripture and tell him that I love him, you won't be able to speak a word.* At that instant I felt my mouth had clamped. Those around me were asking questions, but all I could do was cry and nod my head.

Finally, I gave in. *OK, OK, Lord. You win. I'll do it. I'll talk to the boy.*

Words for Matt

I walked to the kid's table. He still had his head down. My tears were drying, and when I opened my mouth, words now came out: "Hey, I'm Bill. What's your name?" I stuck out my hand, which he shook weakly.

"Matt." He looked away and his head drooped.

"Matt, what's going on? How are you doing?"

The boy raised his head and said, "I'm so brokenhearted and I am crushed."

I could not believe it! Those were his exact words, almost a direct quote out of Psalm 34, verse 18! I sensed a spiritual release in me.

"Listen. When you came in here tonight," I said, "the Holy Spirit pointed you out to me. He's been asking me all night to come over and share a Scripture verse with you. It is Psalm 34:18, which says that God is close to the brokenhearted and He rescues those whose spirits are crushed."

Matt looked like he might cry. "Christians can be so mean," he said.

"Why do you say that?"

"I was supposed to have my first date tonight but she stood me up."

"Man, that hurts. I know how you feel. Is she a Christian?"

"Yeah."

"People do things they shouldn't—we all sin. But it will be best if you forgive her and let it go. Jesus loves you," I said. I put my arm around him. "So that's why you're here alone tonight?" He nodded his head.

"Are you a pastor?" Matt asked.

"No. I'm here to speak tonight, but I'm someone like you, someone who realized one day that God loved me very much. He will never let you down, and He loves you very, very much."

The boy's whole appearance started to change. He smiled. "Can you come to church with my mom and me this weekend?"

"No, I'm sorry; I can't—I need to be with my family back home." We talked some more and I learned that his father was not active in his life. So I shared a little of my story, how my dad had left when I was a baby. "Matt, let God be the father you've always looked for," I said.

I had to go up and speak, but almost right away I noticed some other kids came over to the boy's table. I saw him smiling and talking. God had appointed others to help out too.

I don't remember much else about that evening. I gave my testimony and headed home. It was clear to me, though, that my mission in Maysville that day had little to do with my speech. It was so confirming to have God reveal Himself like this. What an honor to be asked by a loving Father to deliver a message to a hurting boy. In disobedience I had resisted, but when I finally let God use me, He did what He does best—ministered to an aching heart.

I had a choice that night. Even though the Holy Spirit repeatedly nudged me, I could have said no. If I had, I know that later I could have repented of my disobedience and God would have forgiven me. But by disobeying I would have missed a great opportunity to run an errand for the king of kings. And I also would have not seen my faith strengthened in a living, active, speaking God.

Is It His Voice We Hear?

I love how God wants to communicate with us. But how do you know it's God when you hear that whisper in your spiritual inner ear?

This is a critical question, and I admit that hearing God's voice through the whispering of the Holy Spirit is not a "slam dunk" experience because there are many voices competing for our attention. We have the voice of our own random thoughts and our selfish nature—the flesh. Then there are the voices of other people, like our parents or other family members, who over the years have told us all kinds of things that still echo inside us.

The most difficult voice to deal with is the one of our Enemy—Satan. He's a liar and deceiver and we know he disguises himself as an "angel of light" (2 Corinthians 11:14). I don't think it is crazy to believe that Satan sometimes disguises himself as the Holy Spirit. When Jesus was tempted,

He recognized Satan. Yet the Enemy still tried to trick Him by quoting Scripture! Will the Enemy not try similar tactics with you?

With all of those voices clamoring, how can we be confident that we are hearing the "still small voice" of God? We know God wants us to hear because Jesus said, "My sheep hear My voice" (John 10:27 NKJV). And helping us find our way is one of the key roles of the Holy Spirit. We need to constantly seek the Spirit's guidance.

Maintain Your Relationship

Maybe the most important thing in picking out God's voice is to really *want to hear* from God on a consistent basis. If we only seek God's input when we are in pain or have a crisis, then I think it will be hard to hear His voice. Our ability to hear God's voice is intertwined in our relationship with Him. God is a person, and as in every intimate relationship, it takes time and work to understand the thoughts and emotions of another person. If our relationship with Him includes praise and thanksgiving, we are more prepared to hear words of guidance and present our petitions. That's a balanced relationship.

The most obvious place we "hear" God's voice is in His Word—the Bible. I like to tell people, "To know God's voice is to know God's Word." God's not going to say things that directly clash with what He's already spoken in His Word or are in conflict with clear biblical principles. So if you hear a voice say, "I'm leading you out of your marriage," or "This is God. Go blow up Yankee Stadium," you need to conclude, *That doesn't sound like something God would say.*

Of course, there are times when what we think God is saying is not in conflict with His Word, but we're just not sure it's Him speaking. That's when I pray, "God, will You confirm it to me?" I don't think asking for that offends God. In fact, I think He is honored that we would ask Him to confirm what He's already said to us. I believe that when we trust the truth of what God has told us but aren't sure how it's going to happen, asking Him for clarity demonstrates our faith (like Mary with the angel Gabriel, Luke 1:34). But if we ask because we're not sure God can pull it off, it shows our lack of faith (like Zechariah doubting what

Gabriel told him about the birth of John the Baptist, Luke 1:18–20). Asking with faith shows we're serious about our obedience.

If I'm not sure I'm clearly hearing God, and if Scripture is silent on the matter, I try to make sure that everything lines up with His Word. I can also look at circumstances, as well as the advice and wisdom of others. Another good measure is peace. It's wise to ask, "As I decide to obey what this voice or impression is telling me, am I filled with peace or do I feel fear and anxiety?"

Passion for God and complete surrender to His ways seem to turn up the volume of God's voice. The Bible says that when we draw near to God, He will draw near to us (James 4:8). If we are inconsistent in our commitment to Him, it will be hard to hear His voice. It amazes me how clear His voice becomes when we're totally surrendered to Jesus Christ. And it's amazing how distorted His voice is when we're putting our value on things that are not what God wants for us.

It really comes down to our relationship and seeking Him: "For everyone who asks receives; he who seeks finds; and to him who knocks, the door will be opened" (Luke 11:10). God doesn't want to play hide-and-seek with us.

For me listening to God is one of the most fun things about being a Christian. Think about it! We get to have an ongoing conversation with God!

Walking under the direction of the Holy Spirit: It's the only way to go!

waiting

12

The best things come when we obey God by standing still.

When I was a new Christian, it seemed like I had something of a honeymoon in my faith, because so many prayers were answered quickly. Then I found out that the real testing and strengthening of faith occurs when we have to wait on God.

I do believe God hears and answers all our prayers, but many times it takes longer than we would like. That's when we acquire the grit and patience required to follow God through thick and thin. We live in a "McDonald's" society where we want to pull up to a drive-through prayer window, grab our blessings, and go. Or we think that if we can figure God out, there must be a formula to receiving answers to our prayers. But there are no formulas with God. He responds to faith, not formulas.

Faith says, "I'll trust You, God, and wait, no matter how long Your answer takes." A formula would say, "God, You have to respond in a particular way."

In chapters 6, 9, and 10, I told stories about quick answers to prayer requests. God does that at times, but we should not expect that. When God says no to me, He is still answering my prayer, and I have learned to accept His yes and His no. When God answers our prayers with a no, faith accepts that our good God has done what is best for us and for His glory. Thankfully, early on I learned the simple value of praying for my daily bread and being appreciative when God provided and showed Himself faithful every single day. I embraced what Jesus said: "But seek first his kingdom and his righteousness, and all these things will be given to you as well" (Matthew 6:33).

When I was waiting on God to answer, He often assured me that the delay was not because I had a deep-rooted sin in my life. It was all about timing—*His*. The Devil tried to sell me a different story because he's an accuser and a good one at that. He has whispered, "Are you sure you confessed everything? What about all the mistakes you've made with money? Don't you remember how immoral you were?" Satan never quits with that stuff. And he will try to convince you that God never forgave you for *that* sin.

And God will whisper, "You are forgiven! Don't think so much about unanswered prayer. Just pray. I desire to take you somewhere where you can't see or you won't go on your own. I want you to wait on Me."

A Home We Could Call Our Own

One thing God had us wait for was a house of our own. Carolynn and I had always wanted a home of our own, but my irresponsible use of money, much of it lost through gambling, meant our credit rating stunk, and even years after moving from New York City, we were still up to our necks in debt. There was no way we would qualify for a mortgage.

So I was a little surprised the day Carolynn told me of an open house and said, "Let's go look at that house."

We were renting a home in Lexington. I had started a sales job for a telecom company and was making one deal after another, but that didn't change our credit and debt issues.

"Honey," I said, "you know we can't buy a house. We don't qualify for a loan."

"Let's check it out anyway."

To make her happy I consented.

We drove to the house and met the owners, who were selling it by themselves. I recognized the wife. She was the daughter of a man who owned several golf courses in Lexington, and I'd known her when she was younger and working in the clubhouses. Her name was Kelly Fry, and she introduced us to her husband B—that was it, just an initial. Kelly was so excited that someone she knew might have an interest in their home.

We took a tour and when we came to the kitchen, Carolynn gave me that look that says, "I'm loving this." We went to the backyard: there was a heated pool—Kristen would love that. And of course, a fenced yard for the dog. This was the perfect place for us.

Then I was thinking, though, *Houston, we have a problem: I couldn't get a mortgage if I had a gun; no way we can buy a house. Better get out of here quick.*

"I think God wants to give us this house," Carolynn said when we were outside walking to our car. "This is the one we've been waiting for."

Oh no, I thought. But we were trusting God for our lives, right? "I'll go talk to them," I said. I went back inside without a whole lot of confidence. "We really like the house," I told Kelly and B.

"That's great!" Kelly said. "We don't want to sell it to anyone we don't know, because we have put a lot of work into it."

"We love the house, but I don't qualify for a mortgage without a huge down payment, and we don't have that kind of money."

"Why don't you guys move in and pay rent to us, and when you're ready to get a mortgage, you can take it over. Because we really want you to live in the house," B said.

I went out and told Carolynn, and she almost jumped out of her skin. We walked back in to discuss the details and B said, "I do need to get the house out of my name, so at some point you're going to have to get a mortgage. If you have a hard time finding one, maybe I'll owner-finance it for you. We'll make it happen."

We moved right in and it was a great house. But we were still renting and wanted so much to finally be owners of our own home.

An Owner Who Can't Wait

About two months later, B came to me and said, "Listen, I've got to get the house out of my name. Can you get a mortgage?"

"I can, but it's going to cost a lot of money."

"Why don't I owner-finance it?" B said. "Can you come up with a down payment, let's say, about $8,000?"

"Whew, that's a lot. How about $5,000?"

"That'd be fine. But can you come up with $5,000 in sixty days?"

"I'll get the money," I said with more confidence than I felt.

I told Carolynn what had happened and we started praying. We had zero dollars in the bank. We were both working but still living paycheck to paycheck, trying to pay down our debts. This was going to require a major move on God's part.

Pray and Wait, Pray and...

The puzzling part was that we felt God really wanted us to have the place. We had dedicated it to ministry, and we were using it for counseling and praying with people. We wanted others to find community there. We had declared it a "lighthouse for Lexington." After a couple of months, every night when we'd come home there would be five, ten, twelve people waiting for us. The gate to the backyard was left unlocked, and people would let themselves in and enjoy the peaceful setting. Most nights I cooked for everyone there.

We kept praying about the $5,000, but no money came in. We didn't worry, though, which was a bit weird even to us, because we were still uncertain about some things, including our finances. But in this situation, we had total peace. I was doing what I could to raise some cash. I had tried to close some deals more quickly at work so that I could get my commission checks. But nothing had come together. The operative word: *wait!*

About a week before we needed the money, I got the bright idea to call the CFO at my company and see if I could receive some advance commission money against deals of mine that were about to close. I didn't know the chief financial officer that well. She was a lady who had a tough exterior, but maybe she'd cut me a break. So I called and told her what I wanted: The moment I said the word "advance," the CFO laughed. "Advance? Ha, ha, ha. We don't do that in this company. That's pretty funny! We never have; we never will." And she hung up.

I told Carolynn later, "Honey, she laughed at me." In our prayer time that night, Carolynn said about the CFO, "God, I pray that You will supernaturally touch her heart." We left it at that and didn't mention this option again.

We were now down to our last week, and I called and set up a Tuesday lunch meeting with B. We still had zero of the $5,000. Tuesday came and I got up in the morning and, even with a few hours to go, I still felt total peace—and expectancy. God was going to pull something off. As usual I headed off to my men's FCA breakfast. Maybe the miracle would happen there, because so many amazing things went on at these meetings. I would ask the guys to pray for our need.

Before we had the prayer time, David Jeffares stood up and said, "I feel impressed by the Holy Spirit that there's someone in this room who needs a financial miracle today."

Oh yeah! I couldn't believe it! The hair on the back of my neck stood up—this was so exciting. The room was full but I thought he must be talking about me. As I started to raise my hand, another guy jumped in and said, "Man, you are talking about me. I've been out of work for several months, and if I don't come up with a couple of months of mortgage payments, I'm going to lose my house."

Whose Miracle?

Do you see the irony of what was happening? Here I am trying to get money to buy a house, and this other guy is trying to get money to save a house. I've learned that we should never try to box God in: He is full of surprises. And has quite the sense of humor, too.

When the guy stated his need, I hadn't an ounce of compassion for him. In fact, my first thought was, *Wait a minute! That was supposed to be my miracle*! Because I knew a lot of prayers were answered at Tuesday breakfast, my attitude was sinking fast. I was sinning badly. I was coveting. I was jealous. I was stinking the place up.

I did have the good sense to stop the downward spiral quickly. *God, forgive me for sinning against You and this man*, I prayed silently.

While I was asking for forgiveness, all of a sudden I felt compassion for the other guy. It's amazing when you choose to forgive or ask for forgiveness, you take on the nature of God, think clearly, and hear what God is saying to you. Right after that I was prompted to pray, *God, whatever You were going to give me today, give him double.* That's exactly what I said.

The group pitched in and when the man walked out that morning, he had the funds for two months of mortgage payments. I'd never seen that much money collected at a single meeting.

I never did ask the guys to pray for my need. It didn't seem necessary. And on the way out, I went up to the guy who had received the offering and asked him to forgive me, too, for such a selfish attitude.

By now it was 9 a.m. I left with zero of the $5,000, but I still had peace and was full of joy. Once again I'd seen God move in a miraculous way. Nothing better than that. Now there were only three hours left until I would meet B.

Me, Speechless

I drove to the office, and not long after I settled at my desk, the phone rang. It was the company CFO: "Bill, do you know why I'm calling?"

"No."

"I don't know why either, and I don't know why I'm doing this, but I just cut you a check for $5,000, and you're going to have it before noon."

I was *speechless*, a rare occurrence for me. I did manage to mumble, "Thanks."

"You're not to tell anyone about this." She hung up.

The check arrived by courier express at 11:40 that morning. I hurried out the door and met B at the restaurant. We were seated and after ordering I asked B how he was doing. "I've got a question for you," he said. "How do I become a Christian like you?"

"Christian like me? You don't want to become a Christian like me!" I wasn't sure where this was headed.

"No, I want to become a Christian like you, one who's always going to run after God, one who's going to be passionate. That's what I see you doing."

"That is the most important thing—to go after Jesus Christ with all you've got," I said, "but don't follow me." I told him how much we were enjoying the house and how God had provided the $5,000 at the last minute.

"Oh, my goodness, Bill," B said. "That's an amazing story, because let me tell you what I had already decided to do. I'm going to put up the money myself. I don't need any down payment. Take the $5,000 and keep it."

"Whoa, whoa, whoa," I said, "First of all, I can't take that money back to my company. This came directly from God, and if I take it back, I'll walk out of this restaurant and get hit by lightning!" I was kidding, of course, but it was true—I didn't think the CFO would be happy to have me turn that check back in.

"No, you take it and put it toward the house," B said.

"B, this was a gift from God. He wanted us to have your house. You've got to take it!" Reluctantly, B put the check in his pocket.

I could hardly wait to call Carolynn. I don't think we should ever assume God will respond in a particular way. He does things His way and that often is unpredictable.

A Home Worth the Wait

The story did not have its ending until several months later. Carolynn and I went to the company Christmas party in Louisville. Carolynn wanted to thank the CFO in person and said to her discretely, "We know you told us not to tell anyone, but we wanted to thank you for helping us out with the house."

The CFO gave us a blank look. "What are you talking about? I have no idea what you're talking about." I'm not sure why she responded like that. All I know is that God moved, she wrote a check, and we had our house. Carolynn and I will never know whether she was afraid of being overheard or truly was baffled by the transaction.

We do know we were baffled—but not surprised that God had given us the home that went beyond our expectations! He had done it His way in His timing. And it sure was worth the wait!

front-row
seats

13

The key to pleasing God is faith.

The Bible declares, "Without faith it is impossible to please God" (Hebrews 11:6). I wanted to be sure I knew all about faith because I definitely wanted to be a "God pleaser."

What faith really is confuses many Christians. Some think having the right information about Christianity is faith—being able to explain what the Christian faith is. Some think faith is the process of learning about Jesus. I believe that both of those are good elements of faith and even the evidence that someone has faith.

But to me, faith simply means believing what God says.

There are people in my life, Carolynn is one of them, who I believe when they tell me something. Obviously, because we are human we all make mistakes now and then, as do these people I trust. But in the vast majority of cases, I can have full confidence that what they tell me is true. That's how God wants us to respond to Him. He wants us to believe Him, to have confidence in Him, to trust Him. And He doesn't require us to have *huge* faith. The exciting news is that God's mighty hand in our lives is activated by a *little* faith displayed in every area of our lives.

A Big God for Our Big Problems

Such faith is childlike: It simply trusts God for everything in every corner of our lives. I truly believe that is what God saw in David when the prophet Samuel declared that God "sought out a man after his own heart" (1 Samuel 13:14). I believe that David was given that title because he trusted God and had an unshakable faith in God to do the impossible in the face of fierce opposition of bears, lions, Goliath, and enemy Philistines.

David simply believed in God for the impossible. When everyone looked at Goliath, they looked at him in relationship to themselves and they were afraid. David looked at Goliath in relationship to God. Instead of fear consuming him, faith (confidence in God—not himself) rose up in David, and you know the rest of the story.

It is the same with our prayer life. We can tell God how big our problems are, or we can have confidence in God that He is bigger than our problems and start telling our problems how big our God is.

Our faith is like an ignition switch that turns on the power of God in our life. In a car the switch itself is quite insignificant compared to the engine. But without the switch, nothing happens. God treats our faith like that, and it is our responsibility to nurture and grow the faith we've been given. We do that by acting on our faith. James wrote:

> But be doers of the word, and not hearers only, deceiving yourselves. For if anyone is a hearer of the word and not a doer, he is like a man observing his natural face in a mirror; for he observes himself, goes away, and immediately forgets what kind of man he was. (James 1:22–24 NKJV)

Growing our faith is like strengthening our muscles by lifting weights at the gym. As we "work out" our faith, it becomes stronger. Some Christians get this all confused: They think it's the doing or the good deeds that pleases God. That's not it. Yes, our actions are important; after all, the apostle James warns us that faith without works is a dead faith (James 2:17, 20–22). And the faith walk is one of service, using the gifts God's given us. (See Jesus' parable of the talents in Matthew 25:14–29.) Yet our actions by themselves do not please God. It's what motivates our actions—our faith in Him—that pleases God. What we believe (or don't believe) pleases God. And if we believe what He says, we will not be sitting around waiting for something to happen!

Strengthening Those Faith Muscles

I don't want to leave the wrong impression, though, about walking in faith. Just because we believe God and step out to do what He tells us does not mean that every day is a bed of roses.

Through some unfortunate circumstances, I lost my job. This was a tough time because we were still not out of debt from my foolishness back in New York, as well as some other wrong moves we'd made financially. I had also received what I thought was a call from God to enter some kind of full-time ministry, but the doors were not opening. About all that seemed to be happening was that I was broke and owed a ton of money. What was God up to anyway? The mortgage and car payments were piling up, and we were falling deeper in a hole. Honestly, I wasn't feeling full of faith and was discouraged.

I remember one morning in winter when I got out of bed about 5:30 and started praying and praising God. That's always a good way to start the day, I've found. The tougher the times, the more intensely you need to worship. But I also had a question for the Lord: "OK, God, what about *my deal*—You remember—getting into ministry? What do You want me to do? Do You really want me to go into ministry? Or do You want me to stay in the workplace? It doesn't matter to me. I'll do anything!"

I've found that God wants to hear what's on our minds—so there's no reason to hold back: "Look, Lord, take my bills! I need $800 to make my payments. If I don't get the money by sometime this weekend, I'm going to be in bad shape with our car and this house. I'm reminding You of that, because I'm doing this 'cast all my cares upon You'" thing. (See 1 Peter 5:7.)

A Billion Stars

Finally, I got quiet and kept my eyes closed. A picture came into my mind of a clear night sky and what seemed like a billion stars. I knew this image was from God, because normally I wouldn't think about something like this. The thought that came with the picture was: *For every star that you see, that's how many times I'm going to touch you and take care of you. All I want you to do is follow Me.*

"Lord, I'll follow You," I said. "Whatever You want me to do, I'll follow You."

I didn't wake up Carolynn to tell her what the Lord had revealed to me; it was still early and I needed to leave for an all-day training seminar. Keith Frizzel, a good friend from my Tuesday men's group, thought he could get me a job selling insurance for Aflac—the company with the funny duck commercials. I went to the seminar, and when it was over later in the day, I finally had a chance to call Carolynn. "Honey," I said, "God spoke to me this morning and showed me all these stars." I told her the whole story and when I finished she said, "For sure, that was God."

I hung up the phone and noticed something on my shoe. I had put on a suit and a nice pair of black dress shoes, hoping to impress the Aflac crowd. I took a closer look and on the tip of one shoe was a small star, the kind a teacher would stick on an attendance chart. "Oh, man," I said. "You are awesome, God. I get it."

I took that star home and put it inside my Bible on the first page. It's still there, an ongoing reminder of a God who made billions of stars for the heavens, but still makes the effort to stick a little paper imitation star on a guy's shoe—a guy who needs some encouragement to believe that God meant it when He said to cast "all your care on Him, for He cares for you."

Bill-Paying Time

Oh, and about the $800 we needed?

Every Saturday there was a breakfast for men at Southland Christian Church. The next morning I went, as I usually did, and as I came in

I met a guy named Eric. He lived in Georgetown, Kentucky, but attended many services and events at our church in Lexington. I loved this guy because he was a true 1 Thessalonians 5:16–18 man. Those verses are: "Be joyful always; pray continually; give thanks in all circumstances, for this is God's will for you in Christ Jesus."

Eric wasn't weird—he just loved the Lord so much and was a man of prayer. And he believed what he read in the Bible. He often would say, "It's in the manual!" And being "joyful always" is definitely "in the manual."

Now at the Saturday men's breakfast, Eric stopped me. "Bill, I'm glad I found you here today."

"Why?"

"I've been praying for you. God told me to give you an $800 check, and I don't know what it's for, but I think you can use it. Will you take it?" He handed me the check and I thanked him profusely. I remembered asking God earlier that week, "What about *my deal*?" And I remembered the stars—those in the sky and the one on my shoe. And now I had a check for $800—no more, no less.

What kind of a God is this who calls us friend and wants to help us like that on our journey? A fantastic God!

God doesn't always respond to my faith and prayers that dramatically, but I see no reason to back off in taking God at His Word and asking Him to do what He's promised. He has told us that we need to approach Him as children. He's also said that "you do not have, because you do not ask God" (James 4:2). So I am not bashful about asking and flexing my faith muscles.

Fear and Faith

I find that many Christians have more fear than faith when it comes to asking God to honor His promises. It's as if we pray with low expectations, then we won't be disappointed if God doesn't answer as hoped or on a particular time schedule. After all, if you ask for a miracle and it doesn't appear to happen, isn't that a type of failure?—or so the reasoning goes. I think that's a good example of a thought of Satan that needs to be captured and destroyed! It is not our place to critique how God goes about His business. It's our job to have faith.

Don't get me started! But since I am . . . Faith should not be all that complicated. I ask God for miracles on a daily basis. I'm not asking God to do tricks so I can wow my friends. I ask Him to do the things that I can't possibly pull off myself. Sometimes the miracle is "small," like having Him help me resolve a difficult conflict with Carolynn. Or it may be a request for a great miracle—asking that someone I'm witnessing to will receive Christ. Or it might even be asking for some good seats to a concert . . .

Listen to the Band

When Kristen was in high school, she was a fan of the musical group the Dave Matthews Band, so it was no surprise when she asked me one day, "Dad, you have a reputation for getting front-row seats at concerts."

"Sure, honey, I've been going to concerts all my life; you know how I love music. I've been to seventeen Led Zeppelin shows and . . ."

"I know, Dad! But can you get seats like that to the Dave Matthews concert in New York before Christmas?"

And without even thinking, I opened up my mouth and said, "Oh, sure, honey. Why don't we plan a Christmas vacation in New York City. In fact, you can ask your friend Charlotte to come along. Would she like that?" I knew that Charlotte absolutely loved the Dave Matthews Band.

Kristen squealed, gave me a hug, and went to call Charlotte.

Hey, Big Talker

Big talker strikes again. Little did I know what I had done. As always, I was going to need God's help to pull this off.

I started calling my ticket connections in New York where I knew people in the hotel industry and those who sold tickets. I learned these concerts had long been sold out and the going price on the street was three to five thousand a ticket! I didn't say anything to Kristen and decided to wait until we got to New York to figure something out. We arrived in the city a few days before the concert and I started looking. I called and called and called. Nothing doing.

Dave Matthews was so popular that he was doing two concerts on consecutive nights. I gave up on the first night but on the afternoon of the second concert, which would start at 7:30 that evening, the girls and I went down to Madison Square Garden at about 3:30. I found a warm place for them to wait, and then I hit the street.

In my B.J. (before Jesus) days, I would have gone out on the street and found a scalper. *You can't buy tickets like that anymore*, I thought. *You're a Christian now, and you shouldn't do anything that's illegal.*

I figured I'd talk to people and maybe get an idea. One fellow told me, "There's a cancellation ticket line, and last night they let the first 175 people in." I went to the line and saw I was about 200th. I figured if 175 people got tickets last night, maybe I had a shot, so I got in line. Of course, I knew these would probably not be great, front-row seats, but at this point I only wanted to be sure the girls got in. We'd come all the way from Kentucky for this!

I stood there quite awhile, talking to people, watching what was going on. Actually, nothing was going on; the line wasn't moving, and it looked unlikely that anyone would get tickets. It was now about 5 p.m., and this line had grown to wrap completely around the Garden. Several thousand people had the same predicament as mine and I started to worry. I had promised my daughter I would get great seats, and her best friend had told me it was her dream to go to a Dave Matthews show.

An Honest Prayer

I suppose after having God help me so many times with things, I should have remembered to send out my spiritual 911 call sooner. Oh well, at least I did remember. *God*, I said, *I know this concert's not going to glorify You much. But I promised my daughter and Charlotte that we would see the show, and I know that if I don't ask You for help with these tickets, I'm not going to get them.*

It's important to be honest when we pray, and even though we may be embarrassed sometimes that we've got to come humbly with hat in hand, in my experience, God loves these kinds of prayers! I think it's because He knows that we are always in need but often don't realize it. I had plenty of time to pray, so I kept it up: *I'm praying by faith that You're going to get us these tickets, and while I'm asking, I might as well pray for the best seats in the house. And I want to thank You in advance for getting me these tickets. I haven't a clue how You're going to do this, but I know I'll be amazed. In Jesus' name, amen.*

About every fifteen seconds or so from then on, I started thanking God for getting me those tickets.

At 6 p.m. the girls joined me and we stood together in line. The sun was long gone and it was chilly. The line wasn't moving. At about 7:30, the time the show was to begin, the girls started to panic. I told them not to worry—"I'm sorry you aren't in there, but Dave Matthews won't come on until at least 8:30. God's going to come through." And then I shot up some more prayer. *Thank You in advance, Lord, for making this happen. These girls will never forget Your doing what You're going to do.*

Did I have any doubt? Of course, but when that happens, we can follow the example of what the guy who asked Jesus to heal his daughter said: "Lord . . . help my unbelief" (Mark 9:24 NKJV).

The Ten-Minute Promise

At 8:30 Charlotte began to cry. I couldn't blame her; I was starting to wobble a bit myself. This seemed hopeless. Kristen put her arm around Charlotte's shoulders and looked at me with that pleading expression a daughter can give you. "Dad, are we going to get in?" she asked.

I don't know what came over me, but with total confidence I said, "Honey, we'll be in there in ten minutes."

She smiled and went back to comforting and encouraging Charlotte.

As soon as I blurted out that ten-minute promise, the guy in front of me—we had been talking off and on while standing in line for hours together—turned around and said, "I know you drove up from Kentucky to take your girls to the show. I'll be right back." And he walked away. I had no idea what he was up to. He'd told me he was a season ticket holder to all events at the Garden and was standing in line to get tickets for his nephew. In five minutes he was back and said, "I called my broker. I found three tickets for you and your girls. Two tickets are in a section I don't know about. The other ticket, for you, is in the back of the arena. Best I could do."

"Thank you! I'll take them!" He handed the tickets to me and I paid him. "How did you get these so fast?"

"My broker was here, standing around the corner!"

By now it was 8:40 p.m., so I thanked the man again and ran with the girls to an entrance. Kristen was looking at me with a stunned, admiring look—the I'm her "Dad in Shining Armor" kind of thing. The girls were giggling. It was a wonderful thing.

I was thanking the Lord but wondering, *Where are these seats?*

Inside the Garden we looked at the directional signs for the sections, but I could not find where the two seats together were located. I stopped an usher, and he had us follow him. He took us to the front of the arena— "These seats are in a special section of box seats that's on the stage," he said.

The usher backstage looked at the tickets and pointed to the seats, which were about fifteen feet from where Dave Matthews would stand. I noticed there were *three* open seats. I had the girls sit down and I went back to the usher. This is where my New York Italian moxie showed up, I guess. "You see those girls?" I pointed. "They're mine. Here's my ticket; it's in the back of the arena. But there's an empty seat next to them. I know it's a VIP seat, but would it be OK if I sat there? I don't want to leave them alone."

"You sit in that seat," he said, "and if anybody says anything, you have them come talk to me. OK?"

I went out to the concession stand for some cherry Cokes and Twizzlers, and after I came back and sat down, Dave Matthews walked out and started his show. It was great. At the end, James Brown came out and the two performed together. And the girls had an experience of a lifetime.

Tickets from the Father

Afterward, Charlotte, who was not a Christian, asked me, "How did you ever get those tickets?"

"I didn't get the tickets. There weren't any tickets, but I prayed to God for those tickets. You see, God loves us, and like any good father, He wants to hear from us. All God really wants from us is a relationship."

Charlotte looked perplexed. "Really?"

I kept talking. "I can't say that He always gives me everything I ask Him for, but I asked God for those tickets and He gave them to me because He knew how much this would mean to me—and you girls. God loves to do things like that."

I think Charlotte was amazed that those tickets were a result of a loving God answering my prayers. And it always amazes me, too.

I don't pretend to understand the mysteries of God and why He does what He does when He does it. But I do know that God loves it when His children trust Him and ask Him to do impossible things. How many things does God have gift wrapped for us, but we never ask because we think our Daddy is mad or not in a generous mood?

I don't have an answer to that one either. But I do know that without His gracious gift, three people I know would not have sat in stage seats at a Dave Matthews Band Madison Square Garden concert just three days before Christmas.

family
matters

14

*I found out that my ultimate
Father lives in heaven.*

An unresolved issue in my life was the memory of my father and the convoluted feelings I had about him. I had given my life to Christ, but that didn't mean that all my past wounds and problems had magically disappeared.

When you grow up without a father, you have a lot of questions about him and yourself. The worst thing, is you never are really sure that who you are trying to be is the right path to make it in life. It feels like you are in a rowboat in the middle of the ocean without oars.

My mom had always said that I was a lot like my dad. Since I'd learned that my father was a womanizer, gambler, and smart aleck, Mom wasn't flattering me with the comparison.

Mom's family had never cared for my dad because he wasn't Italian. This "negative" had not only ethnic or cultural ramifications but also serious economic outcomes. To be really successful in our community, you needed to be a Mob guy. And to be a "made guy," which in the Mob meant you were someone who's been indoctrinated and accepted into organized crime, you had to be full-blooded Italian.

The Touch of a Father

Even though she was fully aware of all these things, Mom had fallen in love with my dad and they'd married when she was in her late teens. She didn't care, even though her family thought she had "married down." Three children came along in rapid succession; I was the second. Later my dad had some run-ins over gambling debts with the "business" people in our neighborhood. Soon after that, he had disappeared without a trace.

When I was growing up, I wondered what had happened to him and if he might show up someday. *Why would somebody take off and never want to see his children—me—again?* I was plagued by thoughts like that. When I played basketball, I used to imagine sometimes what it would be like to have him come and watch me dunk. I could see him smiling after the game, putting his arm around my shoulder, and saying, "Son—you were unbelievable!" That never happened. I never felt the touch of my father.

Forgiving Dad

No doubt I had missed having a father at home. My mom did the best she could raising three kids by herself in East Harlem. I don't think there are many people who could do as well as she did. But, ultimately, looking back on it, there were consequences of not having a dad there, and those wounds were connected to a lot of destructive behaviors.

I believe two things led to my sin and fueled all my anger, alcohol and drug use, resistance to authority, and a high need for acceptance. First was the bad social environment, including all the emotional and physical abuse, where I grew up. Second was my absent father. Bad things can happen to us in life, but they can be overcome if we have someone helping us make sense of it all and patting us on the back. That's basically what a dad can do—tell you that you have what it takes to make it in life.

I had no one showing me what it meant to be a man. So I tried to learn from the guys in the hood. They threw me to a prostitute to have sex. That was supposed to make me a man. All it did was fill me with anger—that's not how I wanted my first experience of making love to be. Being raped didn't help—that overdosed me with shame. All those wounds festered inside me for years.

During the year after I accepted Christ, all the stuff related to my dad surfaced. Great things were happening to me as a Christian, but there was still something unhealed, because periodically I would get upset. I had bitterness in me dating back to my childhood, and you didn't want to be the one who provoked my smoldering anger.

One day David Jeffares was praying with me at our house on Cave Hill Road, and as he often did, dropped a surprise on me by asking, "Have you ever forgiven your dad?"

"Do I need to? I've never thought I was mad at him!"

"Subconsciously you have been angry at him, because you've lived out the results of him abandoning you."

So that day I forgave my dad, first, for leaving me, and next for any generational sin patterns that he had passed down to me.

Mom and I

When Carolynn and I moved to Kentucky, as I've mentioned before, in addition to our furniture and other stuff, we had hauled along a pile of debt. After becoming a Christian, I found it easier to have faith and maturity in some areas more than others. One of my weak spots was finances. We did not save money. Or we would take a vacation impulsively when we should have stayed home. We could not get on any financial plan because we were always playing catch-up.

We were in a financial mess. But as with other things in our lives, we went to God and confessed our mistakes, admitting we had been lousy stewards of His money.

With our budget tight and a lot of debt, I was all ears when an elder at our church approached me and told of a sales opportunity with a new company. It was a multilevel marketing operation, and even though I had some reservations, I was thinking, *This could be it. I can make a killing, walk away from the business world, go out and share my story and the gospel, and minister to people. That'd be a great life.* I had learned, when considering a decision like this, it was wise to search the Scriptures and seriously look for God's leading. When I felt God's peace, I'd proceed. But in this case, even though the job had some question marks, Carolynn and I still felt an overwhelming peace that I should accept the position.

Inside of me I had confidence that God wanted me to do this—for reasons that weren't totally clear.

I signed on and started work. One of the reasons this company wanted me was to take advantage of my contacts in New York. Almost immediately I started spending two weeks of each month in the city. "Coincidentally," during this same time period, my mother was diagnosed with cancer. I talked to her and my sisters, and we agreed Mom would have the best chance to beat the disease if she had her treatments in New York. Mom was living alone in Florida because my stepfather had died, so she decided to return to the city.

With my new job, I was able to see her frequently during my business trips there. *Ah, that's one of the reasons for my job!* I thought. *Thank You, Lord.*

On one of my business trips to New York for my new employer, as I often did, I attended a Sunday morning service at Times Square Church. During the sermon the Holy Spirit reminded me that I had not spoken to my mom for some time about Jesus.

I need to fill in some background. When Carolynn and I moved to Kentucky and I later became a follower of Jesus, my mother thought I'd joined some hee-haw cult or something. Others in the family gave the same cool reaction. I thought I was sharing the greatest news imaginable—all about forgiveness of sins, a restored and intimate relationship with God, and living in heaven forever—but they thought I had gone crazy and even got upset with me. Their attitude was, "How can you be anything other than a Catholic?"

A Time for Prayer

I tried many times to talk to my mom about receiving Jesus, but she would have nothing to do with it. Mom didn't get what being born again meant or how you could have a relationship with Jesus Christ. All she knew was she'd been born a Catholic, and that meant the spiritual part of her life was covered. She was not active in the church but she saw no need to change anything. I reached a point where I was totally frustrated with not being able to minister to my mom.

Now Mom was about to start a round of cancer treatments. As I listened to the sermon, I wondered, *How much time does she have on this earth?*

Since I would visit my mom that afternoon, after the service I gathered about ten people I knew at the church and asked, "Would you pray that this will be the day that my mom gives her life to Jesus Christ? And she would do this without any prompting from me?" The group circled around me and prayed hard. It was great, and I believed God had answered yes while we were praying.

I drove out of the city and headed upstate to my sister Ann Marie's place where Mom was staying temporarily. As I drove I was so expectant and joyful because of the intense prayer time at church. When I came to my sister's house after an hour's drive, I was walking through the front door when I heard my mom calling.

"Is that you, Bill?" She was resting in her room in the basement.

"Yes, Mom, I'm coming down."

Mom Meets Her Father

When I saw her she looked me straight in the eye and said, "Bill, how can I get closer to God?"

I told her a few things and without hesitation, fifteen minutes later, Mom accepted Jesus Christ. I really didn't do anything except show up! She was ready.

I've said often in talks and sharing my testimony what my friend David Hysong once told me: "When your desperation exceeds your embarrassment, you become a good candidate for God to move in your life." I think that's where my mom was that day, because she had no idea how serious her cancer was. God had responded quickly to our prayers and moved in my mother's life.

That afternoon I baptized Mom in that same basement room.

After further evaluation of her cancer, Mom's doctors told us that her situation was grim—the disease was eating up her bones. She went in the hospital for treatment, but after a month, her health started improving. More time passed, and the cancer seemed to be disappearing through the chemotherapy, the radiation, and most importantly, the prayers.

Every business trip to New York, I would go to the hospital in the evening and see my mom. We would study Scripture together, pray, and talk about God and the Christian life. Mom was hungry for knowledge about her new found faith. She grew rapidly and talked to God about everything. Each day Mom became bolder in expressing her faith.

My Mom's Witness for God

One night when I came for a visit, Mom said, "Bill, let's pray for my new roommate." So we started praying at about ten o'clock and asked God to touch and heal this lady. The next day the roommate's husband came in—he had not been there the night before. "Rosie," he said to my mother, "I've got a question for you. Something strange happened last night when I was home."

"Yeah? What?"

"In my kitchen I heard a couple of voices of two people praying for my wife."

"About what time was that?"

"About ten o'clock."

"That was the exact time my son and I were praying for your wife," Mom said, beaming.

The man got teary and said, "I know now that there's a God."

In sharing this with you, I don't want to give the idea that things like this *must* happen if we are fully experiencing God's presence and power. God works in many different ways with many different people, so how He chooses to work is up to Him. But He is the God of all flesh and *nothing* is too difficult for Him to accomplish. When He moves like this, let's rejoice in His power and grace.

Another time her doctor came for a visit: "Hey, doc," Mom said.

"I've got something that's probably going to make you upset, but I've got this second opinion."

"Really? You're not . . . did you see somebody else?"

"Yes, and my other doctor told me that I'm healed."

"Healed? Who is this?"

"Well, His name is Jesus Christ. He's healed me. So you don't have to worry."

It was so awesome to hear Mom say that, because she'd found out the doctor's wife had recently received a cancer diagnosis. Mom shared her faith in a simple but compelling way that touched him.

I was so pumped: This was the same woman who a few months ago thought I was loony tunes for following Christ.

About My Dad . . .

During those days with Mom, I remembered a day years earlier when I was contacted by my uncle, my dad's brother, who told me that my grandmother was still alive and living in Los Angeles. My sisters and I had never met her, so later when some business took me to California, I contacted my uncle and made plans to see him and my grandmother. During a nice visit with both of them, I found out that when my dad had disappeared in 1961, they had never heard from him again either. It made some sense that a man might leave his wife and family and never contact them. But why would he never call or send a card to his mother?

Years later, as a Christian, one day I was praying and asked God, "Can You tell me what happened to my dad?" The answer that came: *Your mom knows.*

Now, on one of my visits to the cancer ward, I finally found the courage to ask about Dad. "Mom, what really happened to Dad? He was murdered, wasn't he?"

She started to cry and couldn't stop. She obviously knew more than she'd ever told, but all these years later, she still couldn't talk about it. I asked again gently, "Dad was killed, wasn't he?" She nodded her head.

That's as far as the conversation on my dad ever got. I never learned the details, but I suspect because he was a gambler, drinker, and loudmouth, he crossed someone. Mom knew a lot of Mob guys in the neighborhood who would kill someone without thinking much about it. Somebody took Dad out. And any information she had went to the grave with her.

We thought Mom would beat the disease, as she improved with chemotherapy and the doctor was thinking of releasing her soon, as her strength was returning. But after one of her later chemo treatments, she caught a virus that really knocked her back. Her immune system was depleted and she died a day and a half later.

Actually, God *had* healed my mom. She lost her foul mouth and anger. She witnessed to God's goodness. And she drew closer to her family. And four months after my friends prayed one Sunday morning, her final healing was complete—a cancer-free body in heaven.

That Sunday—when the Lord spoke to me and I asked for prayer for my mom—was only four months before she died.

A Job for a Reason

The day Mom died a phone call came from my office in Lexington saying that my job had been terminated. I sensed God saying to me, *The reason I had you take that job was that I wanted you to trust Me so I could use you to lead your mom to Christ.*

In the process I finally learned why my dad had disappeared years ago and put that question to rest. God does things *His* way. That's OK with me.

I rejoiced that my mom had met Jesus and was at home in heaven with her Father—and mine. After all those years of wondering if she would ever come to Jesus, she had! The apostle Paul wrote that when Christians die, they really don't die but "fall asleep," and that we who believe do not need to have sorrow like those "who have no hope" (1 Thessalonians 4:13).

Joy at a Funeral

Her funeral was sad, but for Carolynn and me it was a day of celebration. After the service, my cousin Roseann asked me, "You look like you know something no one else knows. Everyone else is completely dis-traught, but you look peaceful."

"Yes, I do know something," I answered. "I know where my mom is because of a decision she made four months ago to accept Jesus Christ as her personal Lord and Savior."

Roseann looked puzzled.

I went on, "Everyone here is distraught, but I guarantee you, Mom is jumping up and down for joy right now. That's why I have peace and hope. I'm upset, I miss my mom. But I know I'll see her again because of her decision about Jesus."

"Oh, OK," Roseann said. She and I still have great conversations about faith.

I know that so many people have family members who seem totally resistant to hearing the gospel. That may be true with you. I urge you to not give up! Keep praying! Keep asking God to give you the opportunity to say the right things about Jesus at the right time. He's the One who said that He was not willing that any should perish (John 3:16).

Your family matters to God.

plenty
of good
news

15

Whether we say anything or not, we are always telling others about Jesus.

I know many Christians struggle with talking about their faith with others. I guess because I had been dragged out of such a pit, I could not keep my mouth shut! From my first days as a believer, I talked to anyone who would listen about Jesus.

When I met someone, I would simply pray, *God, do You want me to say something to this person*? Sometimes the answer was no, so I would "share the gospel" without speaking—maybe by offering encouragement or making a person smile. I know that what Saint Francis of Assisi once said is true: "Preach the gospel at all times, and if necessary use words."

Some of my encounters were brief, where God would put someone in my life for a few minutes. But I looked for a chance to speak. And if God gave me the opportunity, I took it. One time I came out of a business in Lexington and after I got in my car and started backing up, a bearded guy wearing dirty clothes banged his fist on my window. There was a railroad underpass nearby where the homeless hung out. In the past I would have cursed at him or maybe even lowered the window and punched him, but now I knew Jesus wanted me to take some time with him.

"Hey, you got any money?" he said. "I just got out of jail and I'm trying to get something to eat."

"I think I've got some cash for you," I said, "but I'd like to give you something more than money. I'd like to talk to you about Jesus Christ, if you don't mind."

"No, I don't mind."

"Have you ever accepted Him as your personal Lord and Savior?"

He didn't hesitate. "It's funny that you ask, because all my life my entire family—and even some guys in prison—have tried to get me to accept Jesus Christ. But I've never made that decision, because anytime somebody asks me about it, I get mad. I've run from God all my life."

I looked him straight in the eye and said, "What is God telling you to do today?"

"I think I should accept Him as Savior." His eyes filled with tears because God was speaking to him.

"Let's do it now!" I led him in a simple prayer and he accepted Jesus on the spot. I shook his hand through the window and handed him some money. I've never seen him again.

That kind of thing happened frequently! I knew it wasn't because I was a skilled evangelist; in fact, I was clueless. But I was trusting God in everything and willing to do what He asked me to do. Each morning I prayed, "Lord, today, put me with someone I can touch for You and turn that into a ripple that will affect someone else."

Offensive for the Gospel!

"Sharing our faith" shouldn't be such a big deal. First, you need to want to be used by God in that way—a willing heart is the key. We all need to remind ourselves what's at stake: God and Satan are at war over the hearts of people, but because of the triumph of the cross, we have the upper hand in the battle. We need to plunge in boldly.

I know some people avoid sharing about Christ because they don't want to offend anyone. *Big mistake.* In fact, I think it's offensive that people don't share their faith!

I admit that we must always seek God's wisdom with every individual. I have become so excited about my faith at times that I didn't even think about taking a second to stop and ask, "God, what do You want me to do in this situation?" I rushed ahead of God and, without the Holy Spirit's leading, blurted out things about Jesus and faith. But if the other person isn't ready, obviously, it doesn't work and is offensive.

I've found by trial and error that the key is to use common sense and be discerning. Redeeming lost people is God's deal, so we need to let Him take the lead. If you belong to Christ, He's guiding you through the power of His Holy Spirit. He's always telling you when to do something and when not to do something. Isaiah 30:21 says, "Whether you turn to the right or to the left, your ears will hear a voice behind you, saying, 'This is the way; walk in it.'" He lets us know.

"Hey, Bill!"

On one of my return visits to New York, I spent focused time with my sisters—lunch with Ann Marie and Thea at The Pine restaurant on Bronxdale Avenue in the Bronx. This was the same restaurant where my stepdad had been a renowned chef for years, so I still knew some of the people who worked there. One of them was the head waitress, Delores Cappacelli.

When the three of us arrived, The Pine was packed. Delores was tending bar but when she saw us, she waved and yelled across the room, "Hey, Bill! Where you been, you bleepty bleep?" The always-colorful Delores had a sailor's mouth. I had known her since I was a kid. Her life had paralleled my mom's with rough circumstances to overcome in faithfully raising a family. Her son, Matty, had been one of the three other white guys at Ben Franklin High School, and he and I had played together on the basketball team.

We sat down at our table and another waitress took our orders. My sisters and I were catching up when Delores cruised by: "I can't believe I'm seeing you, Billy. It's been so long. But you've got to tell me something.

There's something different about you that I can't put my finger on. You've changed! You seem peaceful. What's with that?"

After I became a Christian, every time I went back to New York I had conversations like this. I was constantly getting chances to talk about Christ, because there *was* something dramatically different about me. These people had known me during the years when I was loud, brash, proud, profane. I loved it when I got the "What's different about you?" question because it gave me an opening to talk about God. I always said, "I'm so glad you asked!"

That's what I said to Delores. Of course, my sisters were listening too.

"Well, since you asked," I said, "I've turned my life over to Jesus Christ. I've fully committed my life to Him. Now I live for Jesus and He's changed my life."

"Really!" Delores said. "I gave up on Him a long time ago, because I prayed all the time for years and He never answered my prayers. So I told Him where to go!"

Like I said, Delores doesn't hold back. In my old neighborhood when someone said, "Let me tell you where you can go," they were not talking about a trip to Disneyland!

"God's probably very upset with me and doesn't want anything to do with me," Delores said.

Before I could say anything, she flitted off because The Pine is a zoo at lunchtime.

"Tell Me More."

My sisters and I resumed our conversation but minutes later, Delores buzzed back. "Tell me more."

"I've been thinking about what you said, Delores, about God being mad at you and not answering your prayers. Listen, God loves you very much, and all He's ever wanted with you is a relationship. I can't say why God didn't answer your prayers, but I do know that Jesus Christ said that He is the way, the truth, and the life, and that no one can get to the Father except through Him. And what Jesus is saying is that all He wants is for you to accept Him as your personal Lord and Savior, and He will take your prayers to the Father. But He's got to wait until you two are OK."

Delores didn't respond to that but said instead, "Can you pray for my daughter Margo? She has stomach cancer and it's really bad. I think she's gonna die."

"Sure, I'll pray for Margo."

"I gotta go back to the bar." She ran off again.

My sisters were shooting me their "this is weird" look, but we kept eating and talking. After an hour or so we were ready to leave. On the way out I stopped at the bar and said to Delores, "I'm going to pray for Margo, but I think God wants to hear from you today. He wants you to come home and accept Him as your personal Lord and Savior. He wants you to open up your heart to Jesus Christ. Would you do that today?"

"I'd like to do that right now," Delores said. So we prayed. She gave her life to Jesus Christ in front of that boisterous lunchtime bar crowd. We finished our prayer, hugged, and I left with my sisters.

Laughter and Tears at The Pine

Several months later I heard that Margo had been healed of cancer and was doing well. But I had to wait for the really great news. Four years later I was back in New York and attended a festival in Second Little Italy. I saw old friends—some I'd lost touch with after grade school. And to my delight I heard Delores yell out, "Hey, Billy! What's with you? You came back for the free food?" I gave her a big hug, and then I saw Margo. She looked the picture of health. "How're you doing?" I asked.

"I am cancer free! In fact, the church and doctors are documenting my case as a healing miracle," Margo said with tears in her eyes.

"Do you remember that day at The Pine when we prayed for Margo?" Delores asked.

"He had a direct line to God!" Delores said loudly to Margo.

"Oh, knock it off, Delores," I said. "That sounds like something my mom would have said! Sure, because of Jesus I do have a direct line to God! But I don't have a line that's any better than yours! It was your prayer that made the difference, after you got yourself reconnected to Christ!"

We all laughed, and then we began to cry—tears of joy. Hearing about Margo's health, and the answer to her mother's prayer, made that moment one of the best of my life.

A Grace Opening

One more thing I've learned about sharing my faith: *Grace opens the door for truth.* I rarely get into arguments with people about faith topics because I try to demonstrate grace first. Jesus was the master of this: He always welcomed people into His presence with grace.

Jesus' encounter with the woman at the well is a classic example of this way of relating to people. Jesus first asked the woman for a drink, an evidence of humility that disarmed and intrigued her. She eagerly entered into conversation with Him: "You are a Jew and I am a Samaritan woman. How can you ask me for a drink?" As the conversation progressed, Jesus was able to share truth about her life—"you have had five husbands"—and she was not offended (see John 4:4–26). I doubt that she would have hung around the well very long if Jesus had told her first that He knew about all her husbands.

I imitate this approach when I talk to people. I first find out what's on their heart. I really want to know because people are important. I let them know that God loves them very much: "This is love: not that we loved God, but that he loved us and sent his Son as an atoning sacrifice for our sins" (1 John 4:10). People already have enough shame and guilt. You really don't have to convince a bank robber that robbing banks is wrong. What you do need to convince him of is that even while robbing banks, God loves him!

Most people think they have to earn their way into a relationship with Jesus Christ, so the one truth that disarms them is that God genuinely cares for them and has great plans for their lives. This information softens people. I've seen them open up and start sharing things with me they've never shared with anyone else before, because grace has created a safe place to talk.

This is what Jesus did on another occasion with the woman caught in adultery. When the Pharisees dragged her to His feet, Jesus first dispersed the crowd. Only when He had prepared a safe place for her by His grace did Jesus confront her with the truth: "Go now and leave your life of sin" (John 8:11).

I encourage you to relax about sharing your faith. Trust God with this! Ask Him to bring people your way and to give you the wisdom to know when to use words. Love people. Listen to their hearts. Help them find a relationship with the greatest Person they will ever meet.

There's nothing quite like hearing someone say, "Yes, I want to know Jesus."

troubles

16

I learned God is faithful and good even when things don't go as planned.

Jesus wasn't kidding when He told us that "In this world you will have trouble." If that's all He'd said on the topic, we definitely would be hurting. But Jesus concluded the thought by saying, "But take heart! I have overcome the world" (John 16:33).

The troubles we encounter have a variety of causes. Satan and his buddies mess with us and can do a lot of damage if we don't dress in the "full armor of God" (Ephesians 6:10–18) and stand up to them in Jesus' name. Living in a fallen world brings problems. This is not heaven. And a significant troublemaker for me has been my own foolishness.

I've already mentioned how my recklessness with finances before I was a believer led to a large debt. The consequences of those poor choices hung with me for many years. For reasons known to Him, God chose not to ease us out of our financial pinch—even though He sent many blessings along the way and our basic needs were always met. What puzzled me most was that my money mess was standing in the way of entering into some type of full-time ministry. What was God doing? Let me tell you the story . . .

Making Money in a Hurry

I was so excited about serving God as a vocation that I decided to nudge God along a little instead of *waiting* for Him to get me to the right place at the right time. With my usual enthusiasm I concluded my path to working full-time for God was to make a lot of money in a hurry. Then I could quit work and get on with it. Bad thinking. Good thing God is the master at making lemonade out of lemons.

A guy at one of my sales accounts told me one day, "I've got a client from Italy who's starting a new company in America, and he's looking for a director of sales. He'll pay you a great amount of money; I think you could make a million dollars in a year at this." That got my attention.

I found out that this company was planning to introduce a new type of bathroom shower into the American market. The shower had a built-in lightbulb so that you could do a little tanning while showering. This product was already a hit in Europe but had not received a patent in America.

I arranged an interview with the man from Italy, and he offered me the sales manager position. Before I took the job I called some of my business associates and friends to see if they thought this product would sell in the United States. The response was positive, so I resigned from my job and took the new position. I was certain that God would have me sell showers for a year or so, after which I would take the million bucks and run away from the business world for good.

This "great plan" seemed obvious to me, but I wasn't operating in the arena of faith. Instead I was depending on natural thoughts and tendencies and convincing myself it was God. More bad thinking.

We can do one of three things when making decisions: (1) *Do what you want to do*; (2) *do what you think you ought to do*; or (3) *do what God leads you to do*. Maybe the trickiest option is the second one: When you do what you think you ought to do, it might be a good thing, but it isn't right because God doesn't have His hand in it.

Before I started the new job, I asked an attorney to prepare an employment contract, something I'd never done before. Maybe I sensed that something might be amiss, but my new boss signed the contract and I started work.

Patent Pending

There was a detail I should have paid more attention to: When I decided to help market the revolutionary shower, my boss assured me that obtaining the patent was no big deal. He asked me to finish up the patent application proceedings while also marketing the product. I soon learned that the patent wasn't a given and the approval process for the shower, because of the ultraviolet lighting and other safety-related issues, might take years. I told my boss but he insisted that I sell the shower anyway.

I was in a big bind: I didn't want to sell a product and take deposits from customers when I could not deliver. So I confronted the owner. We had a heated "discussion" and he fired me. At this point I was so glad I had signed a contract guaranteeing me a year's salary, because we were still getting our finances in order and paying off debt.

You can imagine my disappointment when the owner informed me he was not going to honor our contract. I went to my attorney and he said I had a great case, but I would have to take the owner to court, which meant expenses for legal work. If I could win the case, our family could get back on our feet financially. But if I lost, I faced financial disaster. We might lose our house and have to declare bankruptcy.

I asked my attorney to proceed and we started taking depositions. Everything looked good, because my former boss repeatedly shot himself in the foot. As the process continued over several months, it looked like we had the case won. It was a matter of time.

I was thanking the Lord for these developments and starting to breathe easier when a friend of mine called and said, "Bill, I don't think you should be suing this guy." She quoted the Bible verses (1 Corinthians 6:1–8) that warn us not to sue a brother in Christ. "Don't you know that you're already defeated if you take him to court?" my friend said.

Oh, man, I didn't know what to think! *What would we do without this money?* "Well, let me go pray about it," I told my friend.

A Grace Challenge

Carolynn and I started to pray, as well as look more carefully at what the Bible said. We looked for any possible loophole in that passage. I admit this is not a good way to study Scripture, but we felt desperate. We wanted to do the right thing, but we also knew that if we dropped this case we would face financial devastation.

My former boss said he was a Christian, but I didn't feel he was treating me like a brother in Christ. That's when God made it clear to me that how the man was behaving or his heart motivation was not for me to judge. I needed to trust God and leave it at that.

This confusing situation was turning into what I describe as a "grace challenge." I believe that some events in the life of every serious follower of Christ are used by God to find out how we will respond. This lawsuit issue was no exception—would we trust God or not?

In the meantime, we were still taking depositions and sometimes I was in the same room with my former employer. I did not feel ill will toward him and continued to pray for him. I did this even though the man tried to throw me into the river. For example, he brought up that I had witnessed to people about Christ when I was on the job and that I had used e-mail to tell people that I was praying for them, which must have meant I "wasn't working." I really wanted to get mad at him, but God helped me not get upset. I kept on asking God to bless him and touch his heart. I was being tempted to hold a grudge against him because he had slandered me. God kept on reminding me to forgive him—the "grace challenge." So I did.

That's when God pointed out to me, *You say you've forgiven him but you're still taking him to trial?* I justified my actions by thinking, *Yes, I have forgiven him, but what's right is right. Just because I forgive him does not mean he should not pay me what is rightfully mine.*

Releasing the Debt

I wasn't getting it: *Forgiveness means releasing the debt.* I had to release this guy of the debt, but I didn't want to. There's no halfway point in forgiveness. Too often we say "I forgive," then right away we add "but . . . " The "but" always gets us in trouble. Whatever follows the "but" reveals that we haven't truly forgiven. Forgiveness is a stand-alone statement: "I forgive you because I choose to forgive you. I've done it from my heart and I've released the debt. No hidden clauses. No stipulations. No 'buts.'"

I find that whenever God's trying to get me to another level with Him, in that period of trial He's always giving me grace challenges— someone is put in my life who I need to extend grace to. Almost against my will, a great deal of compassion came over me for this guy.

After wrestling with our decision, Carolynn and I agreed that God wanted us to drop the case. Carolynn and Kristen were particularly anxious about the possibility of losing our house. I knew how important security and stability were to them, and I kicked myself for taking this job in the first place. But I also began to think that God was unfair. *How could God allow us to lose the same home that He had so miraculously provided a few years earlier?* I was confused.

We went to our attorney, and when we asked him to end the lawsuit, he said, "OK, but it's a done deal. You won't get anything." I did ask my ex-employer to pay our attorney fees, which he gladly did. But we were toast.

What Now, Lord?

We knew we had done the right thing and I had a sense of peace. *But what now, Lord?*

I went to God and said, "I know You wanted me to take this job! What is going on? I'm in a big bind here!" There were two mortgages on the house because I had needed to make some expensive repairs. And part of that second loan had been used to get us out of prior debt. What a mess.

Carolynn and I dug in with our prayers; we were like Job or one of the Psalms writers putting our case before God: "Lord, we know You don't want to take this home, right? You gave us this place! It was a miracle, and look at all the great ministry we've done for You in this house.

Why would You allow this to be taken away from us?"

That was our prayer for a while, which I admit was a sanctified whine. As time went on, God moved us both to another type of request: "Lord, we will not put this house ahead of our relationship with You. Compared to You, this house means nothing. If You want to take the house away from us, great. Because we know where You guide You provide. We trust in You for the answer. We're going to follow You. We are not going to cling to this house or make it an idol. We're going to cling to You."

A Time for Worship and Watching God

Let me tell you, praying that prayer and then sticking to it was tough. Although we knew that trusting God in the situation was absolutely the right thing to do, the stress started taking its toll on us physically and emotionally. We were in a heavy storm, a tough trial. We never doubted God or got mad at God, but the trial was hard to go through. We worshiped God during the whole thing and praised Him even when we didn't feel like it.

And God showed Himself more faithful during this test than ever before.

At one point we needed $10,000 to keep us afloat so there wouldn't be a foreclosure. At a Tuesday breakfast David Jeffares pulled me aside and said, "Bill, I've been praying for you, and I sense you need about a $10,000 miracle, so I'm going to pray that you get it in seven days." He knew we were struggling, but I'd never mentioned an amount.

"Sure, you can pray like that for me anytime you want, David," I said with a grin.

Seven days later a man who was familiar with my ministry called and asked to see me. When we got together he said, "I've been praying for you, and I want to bless you and your ministry with a gift of $10,000." I was stunned. All during this time I had been traveling across the state, speaking in schools and churches. This fellow did not attend any of my prayer groups and had no idea of our specific needs. He truly wanted to bless me and the work that I was doing.

As great as this was, though, the $10,000 held back the flood of debt for only a short time. God continued to provide for our daily needs, but it became clear that even though we were walking in obedience, He was not going to rescue us from our financial disaster. After much prayer, we decided we should file for bankruptcy. I can't tell you how I wrestled with this decision. In fact, I waited probably a year longer than I should have because I thought God would provide some other answer. No helicopter came to lift us out of the dark valley. I made the decision and had peace about it. But I still didn't like what had happened.

"In this world you will have trouble.
But take heart! I have overcome the world."

Is It Time to Move On?

I kept speaking and was scheduled to give my testimony at a banquet for the University of Massachusetts basketball team. We now had two weeks left before we had to vacate our "miracle house." We had done some looking for a rental place to live, but about all we could find with our budget were some small houses. My crew at home was glum. We looked and looked, but all we found was a place similar to what we were leaving, but with a rent way outside our price range. Plus, the yard didn't have a fence for the dogs. And even if we could afford the place, a rental company called Positive Properties was marketing the home, so of course our poor credit record would disqualify us. A large deposit was required—we didn't have that kind of cash. Oh, and an extra deposit was needed for pets. This seemed an impossibility. But we kept praying.

Five days before I was scheduled to fly to Massachusetts, Noreen Jeremiah, a friend who had handled our mortgage needs, called. "Bill, there's a guy in town, a Christian businessman, who heard about your situation and wants to help you out. Before you make a decision on a house, wait until he calls you."

"Great," I said. We were encouraged and prayed about this possibility for a week, but the man never called.

The day came for me to fly to Massachusetts and during a layover in Cincinnati, I called my longtime prayer partner David Hysong. We prayed on the phone almost every morning, and on this Friday I told him how desperate our housing situation was. "If we don't find a house now, I don't know where we will move. We have to be out next week!"

David has a gift of prayer, so as our housing dilemma came down the stretch, I asked him to dig in—and he can definitely do that. David can pray for twenty minutes without hardly taking a breath, so he was going at it while I walked through the airport terminal to my connecting flight. And one of the things David was calling out to God for was that this guy who had promised to call me would contact me soon.

Then it was my turn to pray, so holding the cell phone with David listening, I started in. "Lord, please let what Noreen told me come to pass; we're trusting that this man is going to help us in some way. Lord, our trust is in You. You need to make this happen, so we're asking for a miracle right now."

And in the middle of that prayer, as I continued through the terminal, I bumped into—guess who?—Noreen Jeremiah, the mortgage counselor.

We were both surprised, and I found out Noreen was with friends, going to Florida for the weekend. I immediately ended my call with David, telling him I had run into Noreen!

"I'm so glad I bumped into you," Noreen said. "I just got off the phone with Danny, the fellow who wants to help you. Don't get on your flight! He's going to call you in about ten minutes."

God on the Move

I knew God was on the move, because Noreen had been on the phone with Danny when David and I were praying about the situation. Other passengers started boarding my flight but I waited. The minutes ticked by. I was about out of time when my cell phone rang. "Hello, Bill, this is Danny. I heard about your situation and want to help you out. What can I do?"

I quickly explained our need for a house. "I've been brought up to speed on that," Danny said. "Let me tell you what I tried to do for you. I went back downtown and tried to buy your house back from the banks, but they want a lot of money for it, probably more than what you're budgeted to pay. And I didn't think you would want to take on a large payment now."

I agreed. We needed to stick to our new budget.

"What other options have you looked at?" Danny asked.

"We've looked at a ton of houses, but they're all small and cost $1,400 or more to rent a three-bedroom."

"Any other options?"

"My wife, Carolynn, did find one house, but it's out of our range."

"Where is it?"

"Drayton Place."

"Where on Drayton?"

I gave him the address and said, "This house is exactly what we would like, but there's no fenced yard and it's with a rental property company. It's also way too expensive."

"What's the company?"

"Positive Properties."

"Oh, I own that company. Hold on, I'll call you right back."

Bring the Dogs

The door was about to close on the boarding ramp, and the gate agents were giving me dark looks. My phone rang. "Hi, it's Danny. I don't really have great news, but I'm hoping I may have something to tell you soon. I own 95 percent of my properties, but this is one I don't own. But I spoke to the owner and was able to get the monthly rent lowered by $700. And you don't have to worry about an application or deposits.

"They don't allow dogs normally, but they're going to give you permission to bring the dogs in. If you want the place, it's yours."

What an amazing answer to prayer! We rented the house and were so thankful. A lesson we learned is that even when troubles come and God does not answer our "why" questions, He never leaves or forsakes us.

timing

17

God does things His way . . . perfectly!

Why does God place a desire in our heart, often a desire to serve Him, and then make us wait for its fulfillment?

If I had the answer to that question, you could call me a prophet. Or maybe an author selling a lot of books. Or both.

To me, there is one answer to that question: *timing.* His timing is always perfect. I learned this in a big way as God put me in vocational ministry in a creative way at precisely the right time.

I was still looking for God's path to bring me into ministry, and could not figure out why the delay. I knew God had called me, so why was it taking so long (or at least long to me)? I was learning in a most personal way the truth of Isaiah 55:8 that His ways are not our ways.

Our financial ordeal had left us spent—physically, emotionally, and at times spiritually. Carolynn developed an ulcer. I was depleted and needed a safe haven, a place to connect in a fresh way with God.

During all this turmoil, Carolynn and I went to a Christian concert, where we ran into Richard Gaines, a pastor of an African-American Baptist church in Lexington. I had first met him several years before while giving my testimony to a men's group at his church. I admired Pastor Gaines because I knew he was encouraging his members, who had plenty of their own challenges, to have a widespread impact on their community just as he did personally. Richard invited us to attend a Sunday service, which we did several weeks later.

Finding Comfort at Consolidated

We arrived a few minutes before eleven at Consolidated Baptist on Russell Cave Road. We took a seat and noticed that we were the only white couple in attendance. Because of my experience growing up in East Harlem, such a situation has never been a big deal. With me, because I bore discrimination for being "half Italian," I "got" the feelings of racial prejudice and blended smoothly with blacks, Puerto Ricans—even Italians!

The folks at Consolidated greeted us warmly, and I immediately was attracted to the wild passion of the place—the boisterous worship, the fervent prayer, the audience participation during the sermon. Pastor Gaines's topic that morning was "My Father's House Will Be Called a House of Prayer," and during his sermon he announced that the church was starting Tuesday night prayer meetings. That excited me. I also liked the fact that the service was long! Pastor Gaines spoke for about an hour and church wasn't over until nearly 2 p.m. As we left that day, the people loved on us like they'd known us for years. Five or six people actually begged us to come back.

As we shook hands with Pastor Gaines on the way out, I told him, "That was a really good sermon. I resonated with what you said about prayer."

"Rieser," he said, which is what Pastor Gaines has always called me, "it's funny you said that because God woke me up at eleven o'clock last night and told me to preach on this topic. I had a whole different sermon planned for today." Hmm.

I felt a tug that day to attend the church, but Carolynn didn't. Not being in sync happens to us now and then, which I think is normal for couples. The culture at Consolidated Baptist was a big change for

Carolynn, compared to what she had grown up with and grown used to. Her comfort zone was stretched, but I also saw how moved she was by the Spirit every time we attended (which would be for several months on Sunday mornings). I would not pressure her into making a decision. If and when she was ready to join Consolidated Baptist, we could make a decision then.

Getting Tabbed at Brooklyn Tabernacle

Because of so many great experiences attending church in New York City, Carolynn and I were eager to bring along our friends the Burgens on one of our trips back "home." I knew this would be a "spiritual high"—we'd go to church twice on Sunday—attending Times Square Church in the morning and Brooklyn Tabernacle in the afternoon. We could do the city sightseeing on Monday, then head for the prayer meeting at Brooklyn Tab on Tuesday night.

We had a great weekend and arrived expectantly at the Brooklyn Tabernacle for the Tuesday night prayer meeting. As usual, it was an unusual night. At the beginning, Pastor Cymbala stood up and said, "If you are a pastor visiting from out of town, would you please come forward for prayer?"

Jim Burgen went forward with many others. Pastor Cymbala prayed for the group. "God, today I pray for new assignments for every pastor who's come up here. New assignments that are fresh and new from Your Holy Spirit. I pray that You'll give each and every pastor a new direction and a new assignment with what they're supposed to do with their ministry."

Little did I know that this was a key moment, not just for Jim, but for me as well. God was preparing the way for a new assignment for Jim . . . and my entry at last into the ministry God had called me to.

Getting Ready for the Call

For several months we attended Southland Christian Church on Saturday night and went to Consolidated Baptist on Sunday morning. We loved both churches and still do.

Before long I was encouraged to help with several ministries at Consolidated. I loved it! Pastor Gaines became another one of my awesome mentors and encouraged me to pursue God's call to enter full-time ministry.

Sometimes I would lead a prayer during a service. Man, the people at Consolidated loved to pray! I would stand up and begin, "God, I'm sick and tired of telling You my problems!"

"Amen, brother! Yes, Lord, we're sick of that too," some in the congregation would shout.

"Instead of telling my circumstances to God, I want to tell my circumstances about my God!"

"Yes, Jesus, yes! Hallelujah!" someone exclaimed in praise.

After six months of experiences like this, Carolynn told me, "We've got to join this church!"

We did.

I am so grateful for Consolidated embracing me and the call on my life by allowing me to be a minister of the gospel. To this day, when we go home to Lexington, I get to preach or pray at Consolidated, and the bond of love we have is still growing. I'm especially grateful to Pastor Gaines, who believed in me before I could see it myself. I love him and that church.

God Wasn't Kidding

Now the ministry opportunities really heated up. Pastor Gaines told me, "If you want to serve here, you always better have a sermon in your back pocket." He was a man of his word and sometimes called at three o'clock on Wednesday afternoon and said, "Rieser, you're preaching tonight."

"What? That's three hours from now!"

"So? No sweat—I have a topic for you!"

And I did it. Somehow, with the aid of the Holy Spirit, I would speak for an hour or more, which was about the minimum for a "talk" at this church. But what a great audience! People at Consolidated loved the Bible and hung on my every word, like I was Billy Graham instead of Billy Rieser.

And all that love touched my heart and increased my confidence.

One Wednesday I spoke on the power of prayer and afterward a woman in the congregation stopped me. "You sure got in my house tonight! Don't you ever get in my house like that again!" She smiled. That was her way of saying that the message had really meant something to her.

More months passed and I was asked to become an ordained lay associate pastor.

Are you kiddin' me?

They weren't kidding. And God wasn't kidding either: In a surprising way, I was entering the ministry. But I had a lot to learn.

More with Less

The Lord had blessed me with a new Monday through Friday job, and I was working hard to better steward our finances. One noon I met David Jeffares for lunch and he asked me how my life was going. I shared with him how busy I was. "I put in about seventy hours a week at work and another forty hours in ministry—speaking, studying, preparing talks, and traveling."

"So you're putting in more than one hundred hours a week with both of those?" he asked, shaking his head. "Since you've been called into ministry, now would be a great time to learn you don't need to kill yourself doing God's work. Wouldn't that be a good thing?"

"Absolutely."

"We need to pray that God would do more for you with you doing less. In particular, you're speaking at Western Kentucky University this week, right? Why don't we pray for that speaking engagement. Let's ask God to start doing that right away—His doing more with you actually doing less."

That's what we prayed for.

Later that week I drove up to Western Kentucky University in Bowling Green for the speaking engagement. The meeting started at 8:30 p.m., and a good crowd of three hundred students was present.

I began sharing my testimony, and after speaking for five minutes, I noticed that about half of the students in the audience were crying. This wasn't a tear here and a little sniffling there. These people were crying like babies. *What is going on?* The early portion of my story was not about God at all. I usually tell about the hood and weave in some funny incidents. It's not the kind of material that normally brings people to their knees!

I knew the Holy Spirit was doing a work, and people cried until I finished. Afterward I stayed in the room until 12:30 in the morning, because all the kids who were convicted—a large percentage of those in attendance—wanted prayer! We prayed for salvation, relationships, healing, addictions—a lot of needs. Before I left, a girl came up and said that two years ago she had been brutally raped. She hadn't known there was a meeting this night, but four girlfriends brought her. "While you were talking," she told me, "God healed me and took away my pain and hurt and set me free. I've forgiven that man tonight."

That made me cry.

A few days after David and I prayed, I had experienced the answer: God was doing more with my "less."

Oh, and here's the best part: Within that same week, I received a call from our former pastor, Jim Burgen, who had become pastor of a church in Colorado. He and I had talked many times about my desire to be in full-time ministry. "Bill, do you remember how we used to talk about doing ministry together? I've taken a new job and I want you to be the first person I add to my staff!"

I was about to become a full-time minister of the gospel. Almighty God was doing things His way with His timing.

always
talking
to God

18

For me, prayer is life.

There's something burning in my heart that I must say: We need to put prayer back in our . . . churches!

Prayer is our direct link to God. So why is there so little emphasis on prayer? In our churches we have learned to use multimedia to communicate more effectively. We have built large, comfortable buildings to welcome people and keep them coming. We have created exciting worship experiences with music that fits contemporary tastes. We have made the gospel relevant for today's culture. But in the midst of all of these superb modern ways of doing things, even in a "solid church" you are fortunate to hear one or two talks a year on prayer.

You may call me a shameless "name-dropper," but *Jesus* said that His Father's house would be called a "house of prayer" (Matthew 21:13). As important as preaching is, He never said His house would be called a house of preaching. Or a "house of worship," for that matter. Because of this disregard for prayer, I believe our people are struggling, for they don't know how to access the resources of almighty God!

Prayer Goes with Faith

Instead of prayer being as natural and normal as breathing—a way of life—too many Christians use prayer like a spiritual 911 call: Prayer is a last resort instead of a first response. I think we need to take note of what Jesus' disciples did in regard to prayer. The two most important requests they made of Him were "teach us how to pray" and "increase our faith." After following Jesus around, they knew that prayer and faith go hand in hand. Jesus got results when He prayed. Wouldn't you like to be known as the person who gets results when you pray? I would love to have that engraved on my tombstone!

We spend so much time preaching about what Jesus did over two thousand years ago and that is good. We also hear other good things: "We should be like Jesus." "We are to grow in the grace and knowledge of our Lord and Savior." "We are to take on His nature" and do our best to "act like, speak like, talk like, love like Him." What we hear too little about is what Jesus is doing today and has been doing for the past two thousand years. Specifically, the Bible tells us that Jesus lives to make intercession for us. In other words, He's busy hearing our prayers and taking them to the Father!

My point is that no one modeled prayer better than Jesus, and we need to follow His lead. Let's never stop learning how to pray like Jesus.

Prayer Takes Time to Hear God

As wonderful as the opportunity seemed, before we could accept Pastor Jim Burgen's invitation to join his team at Flatirons Community Church in Colorado, we needed to be sure this was God's plan. In other words, we needed to pray and wait to hear what God was saying.

Carolynn and I flew west and spent a weekend meeting the congregation. I was asked to share my testimony, and after returning from our time there, I was pumped over the opportunity. I had prayed earlier that God would give Carolynn and me direction at the same time so we wouldn't be confused or in disagreement. "So, what do you think?" I asked her.

"Other than a burning bush, what other sign do we need?" she answered.

I smiled and we started packing.

Prayer Is at the Core

By the time we moved to Colorado, after being a Christian for eight years, I knew that prayer was the central focus of my walk with God. I have never gotten over—and I hope I never do—the reality that I can converse, anytime night or day, with *God*. And He listens and responds! This is amazing.

My official title was community pastor but I wore many hats. I helped with small groups and marriage ministry and taught occasionally. I also had a major commitment to the Celebrate Recovery team. In everything I did, prayer was at the core.

I think that prayer should be a mark of any Christian. When we describe another follower of Christ, I think one of the most meaningful compliments we can give is to say, "That person prays." You know you have encountered a person of prayer when you ask for prayer and that person says, "Let's pray right now"—no matter if it's on a street corner, in a coffee shop, at the grocery store . . . wherever. There's nothing better you can do than give someone the gift of prayer.

Almost immediately Carolynn and I met a lady named Connie who had an awesome relationship with God. She was trying to find a new direction in her career and wanted to transcribe legal documents. One day she stopped me at church and said, "Bill, can you pray for me? I need to pass a test to become a transcriber but I've failed it three times. I stay up all night and study, but I get nervous and blow it. I need to pass this so I can make a living."

"Connie, we need to pray that God will do more with the same amount of effort that you have given in the past yourself," I said. As you'll recall, I had learned that lesson myself recently (see chapter 17). "And let's pray that He would give you the wisdom and power to pass this test." We paused in the hallway and asked the Lord for that—"Give Connie the ability and confidence for this test. Be there with her. You know she needs this, God. Thanks."

A week later Connie rushed up to Carolynn and me after a weekend service. "You'll never believe what happened," she said. "The night before the test, I decided to go to bed rather than cram. I got up the next morning and passed it with flying colors. It was awesome!"

Another satisfied customer. Carolynn and I smiled. Now we knew God was answering prayer in Colorado, too!

My Wife's Prayer Request

It always amazes me that so many Christians are not confident that God really hears their prayers and desires to answer. Those answers may take awhile to come, and God is often very creative in how He answers, but prayer really "works." Ever since joining the staff, I had talked about my passion for prayer and how God wants to do amazing things in response to faith. But I was still the new guy on the block at Flatirons, and even some of my fellow staff members didn't know quite what to think when I told my stories of God's miraculous answers to prayer.

In the spring of 2007 the staff at Flatirons Church would make a trip to the Drive Conference hosted by Andy Stanley's North Point Church in Atlanta. One night a few weeks before we headed there, I was telling Carolynn about the upcoming conference and mentioned that one of the speakers would be Charles Stanley (Andy Stanley's father and pastor of Atlanta's First Baptist Church). Not long after that Carolynn told me, "I'm going to pray that you meet Charles Stanley at that conference."

"Why should I meet Charles Stanley?"

"I want you to thank him for what his ministry has meant to me personally and to tell him about my dad."

"I don't know if that's possible, darling. There will be over three thousand pastors there, and Charles is only speaking once."

"I still want you to meet him. I'm going to ask God to arrange that."

"OK." I've learned by experience that when Carolynn settles in on a prayer request, stand back and watch God move! And I knew how special Charles Stanley was to Carolynn because her dad, Shade, had accepted Christ after hearing a Stanley sermon on TV. Shade was seventy when he met Jesus, and his life had changed dramatically.

She was so excited about all this that she told Jim Burgen and Sam, the executive director of ministries, "I'm praying that God will open up an opportunity for Bill to meet Charles Stanley, so if you meet Dr. Stanley, make sure you give Bill a chance to talk to him!"

The day after we arrived in Atlanta, the entire crew went to a large P. F. Chang's restaurant for lunch. The place was packed, and seven or eight of us jammed into a large oval booth in one corner of the Chinese restaurant. We were considering menu choices when I looked across the restaurant and was blown away. A man on the opposite side looked like—you guessed it—Charles Stanley.

Encounter in Atlanta

I walked up by the restaurant's entrance to get a better view—it was Dr. Stanley. I pulled out my cell phone and called Carolynn: "Honey, we're at lunch, and you'll never believe who's here."

"Charles Stanley?"

"Bingo!"

"Well, don't go over and say anything, because you'll blow it. Go back to your seat, and if God wants you to meet him, He'll make it happen."

"Yes, ma'am! I'm going back to our table and I'll stay right there." It was not easy for me to not go right over and introduce myself to Charles—I'm type A all the way. But I was a good boy and went back to the table. I had a seat at the end of the booth, though, where I could keep an eye on Dr. Stanley.

"You'll never believe who's here!" I said to the other staff members.

Sam looked at me and said, "Charles Stanley, isn't it?"

"You got it. He's at a table way on the other side of the restaurant."

"Carolynn said you were going to meet him," Sam said.

"I want to let you guys know," I said. "Don't be surprised if I have a conversation with Charles Stanley today!"

Our food was served and while we were still eating, Charles Stanley stood up, put his napkin on the table, and started walking across the restaurant. There were hundreds of diners, but Charles acknowledged no one and made a straight path to our booth. He approached me and said,

"Son, tell me who you are, where you're from, and why you're here?" He reached out his hand and we shook.

"I'm Bill Rieser. I'm a pastor from Colorado, and I'm here for the conference and to hear you speak."

"Introduce me to everyone else," he said. I went around the table and introduced everyone; we exchanged pleasantries for a few minutes. "Thank you for taking time with me today," Charles said, and then he said good-bye and headed back toward his table.

"My goodness. That's unbelievable!" one of our guys said.

I picked up my cell phone and called Carolynn: "Honey, you'll never believe what happened."

"Charles came up and spoke to you, didn't he?" she said.

"Yeah! And he shook my hand and I introduced him to everyone else. It was incredible!" As I was still grinning and giving her the details, I felt a tap on my shoulder. I turned and saw Charles Stanley standing behind me. "Can I talk to you some more?" he asked. "I think we're supposed to have a conversation." I almost leaped out of my chair.

Carolynn's Conversation with Dr. Stanley

"Hold on, Carolynn, it's Dr. Stanley," I said on my phone.

"Listen, Dr. Stanley, my wife prayed that you and I would meet. Could you talk to her?" I handed him my cell phone.

Carolynn told me later that she explained to Charles how her dad had accepted Christ while watching one of his TV programs. She also told him how I was a strong believer in the power of prayer and that meeting him would encourage me.

The two were on the phone for about five minutes. When the call ended Charles handed me the phone and said, "I wanted to make sure that it was your wife!" He laughed. We talked for a couple of minutes, and I did feel encouraged. Then he left.

I saw smiles around the table and some shaking of heads. What a demonstration of the power of prayer to my new coworkers!

I don't think people sense the greatness of God today as much as they used to, so I think God uses incidents like this to reveal both His presence and His involvement in big and small things. This whole incident was an answer to prayer and showed how God wants to know us intimately and participate in the details of our lives. He gives us dreams and works to help us achieve them.

I also think God wanted to give Carolynn the delight of a conversation with Charles Stanley. That's the kind of "little" surprise any loving Father likes to spring on His child.

when all
is said
and done

19

The cross is what matters.

When God moved us to Colorado, we knew two things instinctively in our hearts: (1) our primary mission was to encourage the staff and the people at Flatirons Church in the areas of prayer and faith; and (2) our assignment there was temporary.

After about eighteen months I was asked by our old friend Mike Breaux if I would be interested in leading the recovery ministry at his church, Heartland Community, in Rockford, Illinois.

Once again we prayed and went for a visit. This was definitely a position made in heaven for me. Ever since my own conversion, I have loved helping other people find Jesus, experience His healing of past wounds, and get on the godly path away from sinful, self-destructive behaviors. That's the passion God placed in me. We loved our work and the people in Colorado, but Heartland seemed the place, finally, where all of my experiences, desires, and God's plan for ministry could intertwine. Both Carolynn and I agreed that this was a prompting from the Lord, and I said yes. We moved in November of 2007.

The Race for Grace

I determined early on in my walk with Christ that next to God, the top priorities in my life would always be Carolynn and Kristen. I wasted too many years in my marriage and family to take any chances on fouling up the greatest blessing of all—the people who God gave me to love above all others. So even now in ministry, Carolynn and Kristen have my irrevocable permission to interrupt me at any time. It doesn't matter if I am in the middle of a sermon. If my phone buzzes and I see that it's one of "my girls," I will pause the sermon and answer the phone. If either one needs me, I will excuse myself from the platform and be on my way. That's how strongly I feel about their place in my life.

Carolynn continues to be my right arm in ministry, and Kristen is completing a degree in elementary education. For years she has worked in the children's ministry of her church. She loves God and seeks to follow Him with all her heart and strength. Carolynn and I could not be more proud of her or more thankful to God for how He has walked beside Kristen through the turbulence of our family life.

As for Carolynn and me, we are doing great. We love each other more than ever. In fact, we have made a deal with each other: We try to love each other more today than we did yesterday. We also participate in what we call our "race for grace," which means that when we have a disagreement (We still have them—we're married!), as soon as one person says, "I'm sorry, will you forgive me?" the argument is over. At that point we reconcile and move on. It's not always easy, but we've invested a lot in rebuilding our marriage. Why waste any time on holding a grudge and bitterness when forgiveness is so freeing and harmony is so fun?

"The race for grace" is not a formula. It doesn't try to evaluate who is wrong. We know the value of experiencing God's grace extended to us. We are to forebear and forgive, just as Christ has forgiven us (Ephesians 4:32).

That doesn't mean Carolynn and I don't talk about what happened. We talk, but the first one to come to their senses says, "I just blew it. Will you forgive me?"

The simplicity of forgiveness bothers some people. You can't analyze who is wrong. You just have to forgive the other person.

We both recognize that the relationship we have now, and the love we have for each other, would not have been possible if we had not gone through all of the struggles. We would never recommend such a path to achieve a strong marriage, but in our case, the struggles were all God had to work with.

With our history, it's not surprising that we do a fair amount of marital counseling. There's almost no crisis facing a couple that Carolynn and I can't identify with. We use our story to encourage husbands and wives and to convince them that with God's involvement in a relationship, all things truly are possible.

Our Growing Marriage

And we continue to add more chapters to our marital story. When we were still in Colorado, Carolynn and I were on our way to meet a couple at Starbucks for a time of sharing and counsel. On the drive to the coffee shop, we got into a bad argument. I mean, this was not pleasant, and we said some terrible things to each other without using the exact nasty words, if you get my drift.

By the time we walked into Starbucks, neither of us was within a mile of winning the "race to grace." We were both steaming and not budging an inch. After about ten minutes of trying to put up a good front, I said to the couple, "Hold it. Time-out. Carolynn and I had a bad argument on the way here and we've not reconciled."

I turned to my wife, who had been listening as I tried to give counsel. "You know what? I just blew it. Will you forgive me, honey?"

We talked through a few things and what we needed to do. Then we got ourselves back on track. Now we could smile at each other and get on with helping our friends, who were watching us with puzzled expressions. We try as much as possible to be real!

Of all the incredible things I've seen God accomplish, our growing marriage and a healthy family are the greatest miracles I've witnessed.

Your Faith Adventure

So, how about you? Where are you on your faith adventure?

When all is said and done, at the cross everything was taken care of so we can experience an unbelievable life here on earth. It is not a life without trouble, sacrifice, and suffering. But it should be a life of incredible adventure, excitement, surprise, joy, power, and even fun. Think of it—on a moment-to-moment basis, we have the opportunity to converse with *God* and participate in His great plan for the advancement of His kingdom.

If you have not begun that faith adventure by asking Jesus into your life (see page 64, chapter 6), I again invite you to say that prayer and begin your personal relationship with God. Once we've entered into that relationship with God and His Son, Jesus, we each can play a key role in the greatest story of all time. Yet too many of us—all of us at one time or another—end up acting like we're a little bored. We certainly are not ordering any mountains to move, like when Jesus said to His followers: "I tell you the truth, if you have faith and do not doubt, not only can you do what was done to the fig tree, but also you can say to this mountain, 'Go, throw yourself into the sea,' and it will be done. If you believe, you will receive whatever you ask for in prayer" (Matthew 21:21–22).

I often tell the story of two boys in the early 1900s who bought tickets for a voyage from Europe to America. They were poor and had barely enough money for a ticket to get on the ship. The voyage was to last a couple of weeks, but they had scraped together only enough food to last a few days. When their supplies ran out, for some foolish reason, they decided to hide on a lower deck. It never occurred to them that they might ask for food or help. So, for about ten days, they hid themselves. And grew very hungry.

The day the ship was scheduled to dock in America, the captain toured the ship and found the two boys. He asked them what they were doing. "Are you stowaways?" The boys told him their story, of how they had saved enough money to buy a ticket for the trip but did not have enough money for meals. When they'd run out of food, they hid.

The captain shook his head and told the boys that their ticket included all meals. If they had asked, they would have been fed like kings during the entire trip.

How many of us Christians are like those boys—living beneath our privileges as children of God because we never dare to ask?

A Different Kind of Friday Night

On a Friday night in my pre-Jesus life, I would have been hitting the bars and trying to sneak in a visit to one of my secret girlfriends. And probably having another fight with Carolynn.

Now on a Friday night in Rockford, Illinois, Carolynn and I both will head over early to Heartland Community Church to lead the Celebrate Recovery ministry. Several hundred people, all in various stages of recovering from past hurts and embracing the forgiveness from sin and healing that Christ offers, will gather to share a meal, hear God's truth, connect in groups, and hang out with friends.

A Miracle in the Making

I will speak on a topic but, inevitably, the message will head toward the basics I have shared in this book: Trust Christ. Believe in a God who wants to do great things through you that exceed your imagination. Talk to Him all the time about everything. Fasten your seat belt because you can't know where He may take you—which is OK, because God is good and loves you very much.

Like all of us who have been rescued by Christ, you are a miracle in the making.

My journey continues, an ongoing experience of having God reveal Himself. For me every day is a day of miracles, not necessarily a day of supernatural stuff.

Jesus said that only an evil and adulterous generation is always looking for a sign. The miracle I look for every day is Jesus at work in others and me.

He wants that for you too.

Go live your miracle!

epilogue

"Is Dad there?"

Carolynn and I were in bed one summer evening when the phone rang. It was Kristen, age fifteen, calling from a youth camp she was attending. A small wave of anxiety rushed through me because when Kristen called, normally she wanted to talk to her mom. *What was going on*? It wasn't that Kristen and I didn't have a good relationship and didn't talk, but most of the time the two "girls" in my family really enjoyed chatting with each other.

Carolynn handed me the phone and I braced myself. "Hi, honey. What's up?" I asked. I heard some sniffling from the other end.

"Dad, I had to talk to you." She choked out the words.

"Kristen, baby, what's wrong?"

"Nothing's wrong, Daddy. I've done some thinking since I've been at camp, and I wanted to tell you that I now understand how much you love me. And I also know now that God loves me even more! And I love you both. That's what I wanted to tell you, Daddy. I love you—gotta go."

And that was it, a conversation I'll never forget.

I have told in this book of many incredible answers to prayer, exciting encounters with the living God, miracles, and splendid mercies and blessings that I believe flow from heaven as a mighty river. But the one thing that means the most to me is how, as a result of God's miraculous intervention in my life, the Rieser family belongs to God's family.

When she called that night, Kristen was revealing that in her own time and way, she, too, was accepting God's grace and following the spiritual trail marked out by her parents.

As Carolynn and I began our long journey back from a wrecked marriage, we knew it was up to us to work hard on our relationship, but we had no idea how our daughter, Kristen, would respond to the earthquake of spiritual change she was witnessing. Kristen had experienced first-hand the chaos in our home. She had heard the angry words, the accusations, the slamming doors. She had every reason to hold on to her own skepticism about whether any change in her dad was real or another in a long list of deceits.

Not long after that memorable call from Kristen, she was asked to write a paper for a high school class in which she expressed her philosophy of life. She wrote a strong defense of her Christian faith and among many other things said, "Life is more than this mere little experience on earth. One out of one of us will die. There is no way of escaping it. This earth is not our permanent home. We were meant to live with God and that is why our souls long for something to fill us, but when it is something other than God, it will never satisfy."

Kristen, you are so right. How well I know.

As I write this paragraph, ten years have passed since that night when I stopped running away from God and ran toward Him instead. Back then I was at the end of my rope. My marriage was gasping for breath and I was about to lose my family. I was a tight ball of fear, anger, and bitterness. I was captive to lust and addicted to whatever substance would ease the pain. I could put on a good show for the world to watch, but on the inside I was thirsty and hungry, a burned-out man slowly descending to destruction.

Then I gave my life to Jesus and God began His miracle in me. No question about it, I'm truly a Psalm 40 guy:

> I waited patiently for the Lord;
> And He inclined to me,
> And heard my cry.
> He also brought me up out of a horrible pit,
> Out of the miry clay,
> And set my feet upon a rock,
> And established my steps.
> He has put a new song in my mouth—
> Praise to our God;

> Many will see it and fear,
> And will trust in the Lord. (40:1–3 NKJV)

The reason I believe so fervently in a mighty, active, communicating God who still does incredible things today is that I have seen a miracle close-up—*me*.

No more White Jesus.

Only Jesus.